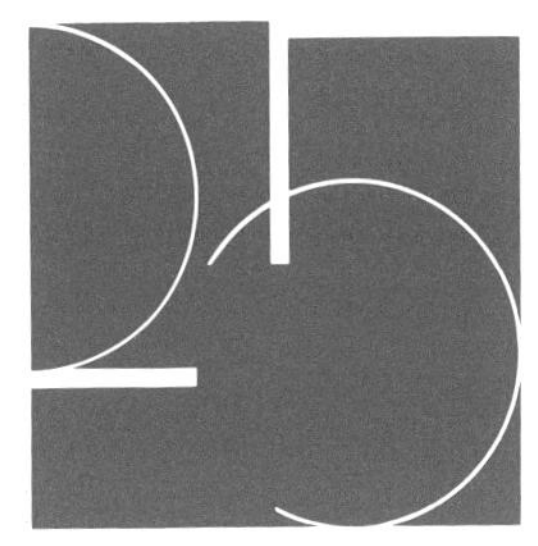

THE HUNTINGTON AT 25

the gallery collects, selected acquisitions 1983–1987

EDITED BY ERIC S. McCREADY

ARCHER M. HUNTINGTON ART GALLERY
COLLEGE OF FINE ARTS
THE UNIVERSITY OF TEXAS AT AUSTIN
MARCH 11–APRIL 17, 1988

Printed in the United States of America.

ISBN: 0-935213-12-0

COVER ILLUSTRATION: Giovanni Antonio da Brescia, Italian, active ca. 1490-after 1525, *The Triumph of Caesar: The Elephants*, after Mantegna, ca. 1490–95, engraving. Archer M. Huntington Museum Fund, 1987.47.

CONTENTS

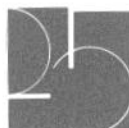

Archer M. Huntington Art Gallery, permanent collection, second floor Ransom Center Gallery

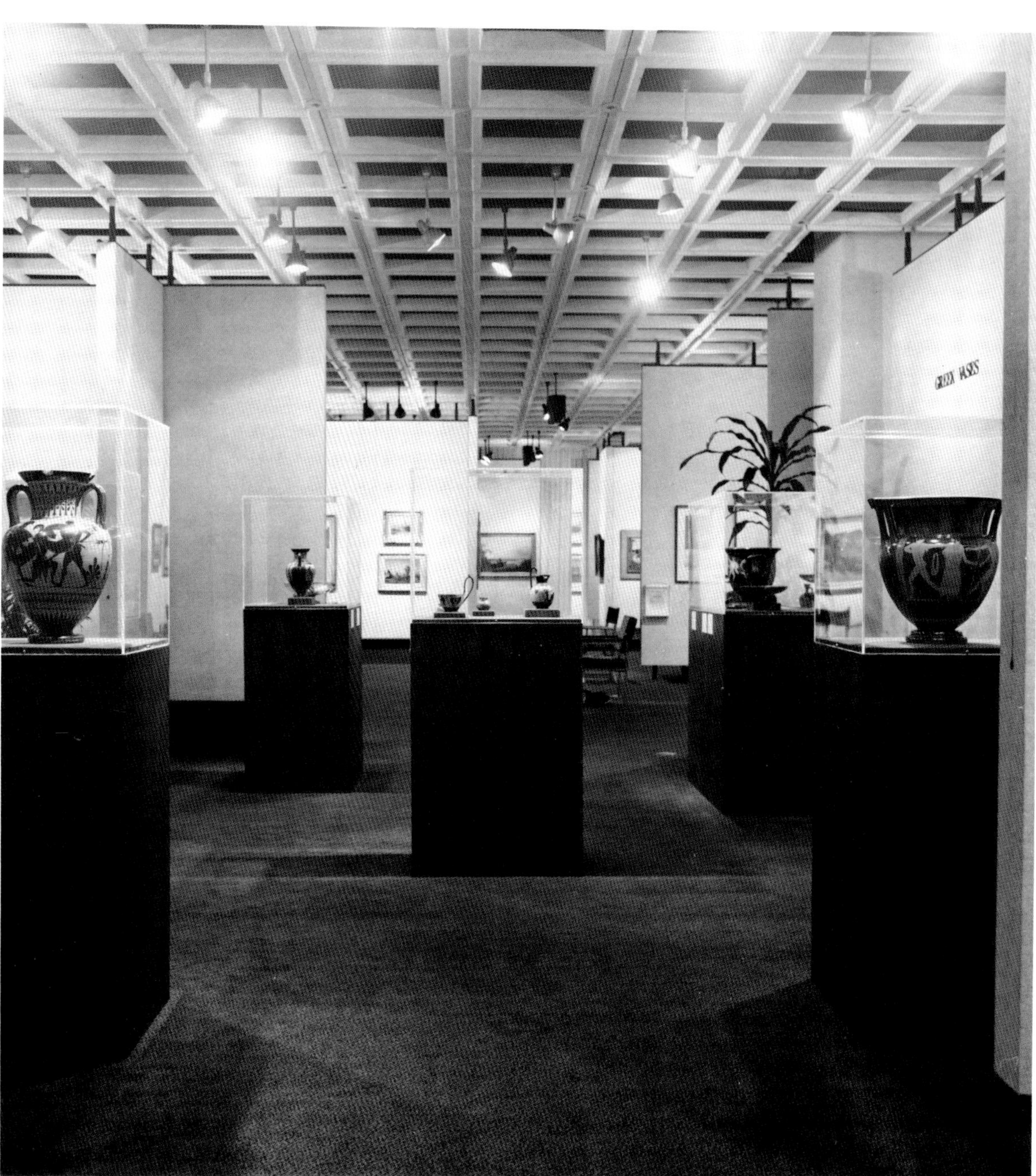

INTRODUCTION

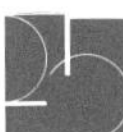

To mark the 25th anniversary of the founding of the Archer M. Huntington Art Gallery at The University of Texas at Austin, the museum proudly presents a carefully selected exhibition of works of art acquired between 1983 and 1987, *The Huntington at 25: The Art of Collecting*. This exhibition focuses on those periods and media within the Huntington's permanent collection which are indicative of its strengths and future directions.

An art museum's image and reputation are reflected primarily by the distinguished quality of its permanent collection. When all is said and done—directors and curators have moved on, public programs are over, research and publication have been completed—what remains is the very heart and soul of an art museum, the works of art themselves. Everything which takes place in an art museum—exhibitions, public programs, conservation, research, and publications—all revolve around the permanent collection.

For twenty-five years, visionary art collectors and those interested in ideas and in the quality of cultural life from throughout the United States have contributed to the on-going growth and improvement of this museum's holdings. To its everlasting credit, the Huntington has continued to focus on specific collecting areas begun early in its history; namely, art of the Americas, from both of North and South America, as well as their European antecedents. These collections have grown under the supervision of a professional staff, trained in art history, knowledgeable of the art market, with the courage of their beliefs, and willing to use their eyes in the search for quality above all, to make the Huntington one of the ten best university art museums on an American campus.

Now in 1988, the Huntington's collection development policies are pinpointed specifically toward twentieth century American and Latin American achievements, never forgetting the importance of their European predecessors from the ancient, medieval, Renaissance, baroque, rococo and more recent periods. During the past ten years, the collection has grown by 3810 objects under sound curatorial and scholarly guidance. Between 1983 and December 1987, 1140 new works have been accessioned into the following categories: prints and drawings, Latin American art, American art, European art, and the decorative arts. Because of the ever improving quality of the permanent collection, requests for loans, both national and international, grow accordingly and the Huntington lends worldwide for programs as diverse as international exhibitions on the one hand, and the United States Government sponsored "Art in Embassies" program on the other.

As new curators come to the Huntington with their own specialized interests dovetailing with the mission and goals not only of the museum but also with those of the most user conscious academic departments, their expertise aids in the development of the permanent collection. Community support has also kept pace with the growth of the permanent collection as students and citizens of Austin and Central Texas come more and more frequently to the Museum to look at art, listen to lectures, and participate in tours and the on-going cornucopia of public programming. What follows is not simply a catalogue thanking our donors or giving museum staff credit for work well done. Rather, brief essays by our curators explain why certain objects have been acquired, what the rationale has been for acquiring them for the permanent collection, and how they serve to strengthen the Huntington as a scholarly teaching and re-

The artist Grace Hartigan lecturing on her work to Art Enrichment students during the exhibition *Action/Precision: The New Direction in New York, 1955–60*, January 1986.

search instrument for The University. These essays will show collectively that when quality is the key, acquisitions are not made willynilly, but are carefully thought out based on long-range objectives and standards which can be set only by museum professionals. In the competitive, national and international art market, with only limited funds available, the Huntington has made remarkable strides forward. Curators, being the acquisitive individuals they are, exist in a competitive environment in which finding and somehow funding new objects for The University of Texas at Austin has become a primary goal.

There is no great mystery about how art museum's acquire new work and one of the goals of this exhibition and catalogue is to demystify the acquisition process itself. In 1981, the Association of Art Museum Directors in its revised *Professional Practices in Art Museums* specified the typical procedure for the acquisition and gift of works of art:

> "The Director must submit for the Board's approval all recommendations for acquisition through purchase.No object may be considered for purchase without the Director's consent. While the final decision rests legally with the Board, it should approve no acquisition without full knowledge of the Director's opinion and, as required by Museum policy, that of the Curator concerned.

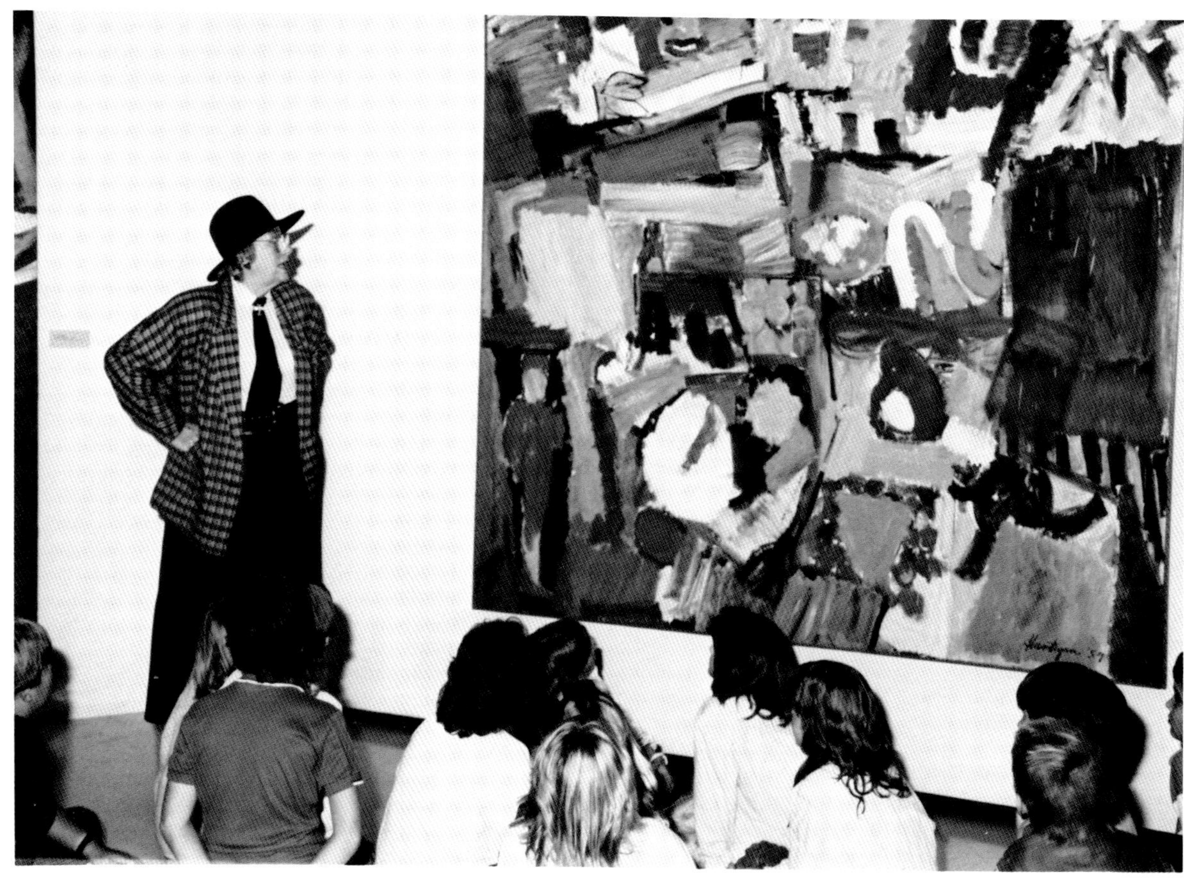

Technical crew installing Santi di Tito's painting, *Rebecca and Eliezar at the Well*, as part of the permanent collection of the Archer M. Huntington Art Gallery in the Ransom Center.

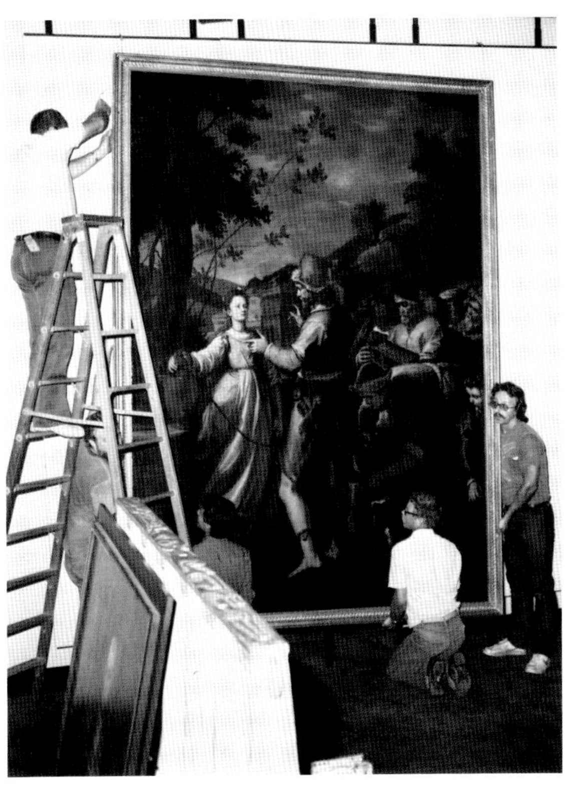

This procedure is particularly important in the case of purchases, since they represent the expenditure of monies committed to public trust for which the Board is responsible. The one exception to this procedure may be purchases from discretionary funds made available to the Director and the Director's staff for this purpose, said acquisitions to be reported to the Board.

A similar procedure should be followed for gifts offered to the collection. While circumstances may dictate some necessary deviations, it is strongly advised gifts and bequests be of a clear and unrestricted nature and that no work be accepted without a guarantee in perpetuity of an attribution or the circumstance of exhibition." (*Professional Practices in Art Museums*, American Association of Museum Diretors, 1981, p. 11).

Since the Huntington does not have a Board of Trustees, the legal ownership and acceptance of all works goes through both the Office of the President and eventually the Board of Regents, which accepts final responsibility and public trust for all art accepted by The University of Texas. Given this professional practices code, it must be remembered that works of art found by curators are carefully studied and reviewed with individuals on the campus who teach specific academic content long before they are presented to the Art Accessions Committee for consideration. The Art Accessions Committee itself, appointed annually by the President of The University of Texas, is made up of five individuals: one each from Art History and Studio Art, two faculty members-at-large from the academic community, and the Director of the Huntington Art Gallery who chairs the meetings. Ultimately, final responsibility for presenting objects for consideration rests with the Director after they have been reviewed in depth by recommending curators.

Since the Director of the Huntington is responsible not only for curatorial and scholarly activities but also for daily operations as well, given the long-range plans which exist in every art museum, it falls to the Director to make the ultimate decision based on the above information. Because extremely limited financial resources are currently available for acquisition, (the State of Texas provides no financial support for acquisitions), if the work of art is sufficiently important, the Director must both commit precious internal funds and raise additional support from the private sector to keep the acquisitions program alive.

There is no way to over-emphasize the

importance of the art museum's permanent collection. Just as a library must continue to acquire books for study, an art museum must continue to acquire works of art for teaching, research, and eventual publication. After all, a permanent collection is the very raison d'etre for an art museum's existence. If The University of Texas at Austin wants a truly great art museum, resources beyond the confines of the Huntington and the College of Fine Arts must be made available. With time and vision, a broad realization of the importance of ideas in the Humanities and Liberal Arts will gain equal parity with those tauted in other academic, perhaps more scientific, disciplines.

I urge you to read, to look, and to enjoy this exhibition, one reflective of achievement and careful deliberation based on excellence and quality.

Eric S. McCready
Director

COLLECTING FOR THE GALLERY

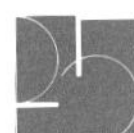

An art museum was first proposed for The University of Texas in 1927, when Archer M. Huntington, son of the railroad magnate Collis P. Huntington, donated over 4000 acres of land along Galveston Bay "to be dedicated to the support of an art museum." The gift of land coincided with the donation to The University of a major work, *Diana of the Chase*[1] by Huntington's wife, the well-known sculptor Anna Hyatt Huntington. Mr. and Mrs. H.J. Lutcher Stark, the donors of *Diana*, had in 1925 given The University a reduced cast of Hyatt's famous *Joan of Arc*,[2] the monumental version of which is on Riverside Drive near 90th Street in New York City. No doubt other works of art had been given to The University in earlier years, but these two bronzes prompted the recognition by Huntington that Texas needed an art museum. The income from Archer M. Huntington's donation of land still funds most of the museum's exhibitions, publications, and acquisitions, as well as (in recent years) about half the staff salaries.

The Huntington donation had little effect in the next years, perhaps as a result of the Depression, or perhaps because the administration was deeply involved in the Master Plan for The University and its designs by architect Paul Cret. It is peculiar, however, that the Master Plan did not include an art museum building; a museum for history and natural history, the Texas Memorial Museum, *was* begun in 1936, in celebration of the centennial of Texas independence.

The College of Fine Arts and the art department were founded in 1938, and rather soon the need for exhibition space became evident.[3] Early exhibitions were held in the Regents Room on the second floor of the Main Building. These ranged from faculty and student exhibitions and travelling shows to exhibitions of color reproductions when original art was not available. During a period when the Regents Room was unavailable, a small space in the temporary art building was used, then the patio corridor of the first music building. There was no permanent collection, but in these years the department did receive some WPA art.

The Art Building, with its gallery space, was dedicated on November 15, 1963, twenty-five years ago. Some of the income from the gift of Archer M. Huntington helped to finance construction of the building, and the rest of the endowment was allocated to support the museum programs. Dr. Donald Goodall, director of the museum in these early years, decided that the Huntington Fund was not large enough to support both a substantial acquisitions program and an exhibition schedule, so the gallery emphasized exhibitions. Since the professors of art history and studio art focused on contemporary American and Latin American art, the exhibition program also focused on those areas, although some non-contemporary art was shown.

Nevertheless, acquisitions were made. Gifts came in celebration of the opening of the building; some prints were purchased, and others were donated. C.R. Smith began to donate his Western collections and Charles Clark began to donate almost 800 prints, making the core of the contemporary collection in the Clark Print Room. The donation of the Tonkin and Romansky collections included some earlier prints. With the 1969 gift by Mr. and Mrs. James Michener of contemporary paintings, the collections of the museum had grown to the extent that the Art Building gallery was inadequate to display or store them.

In 1972 the Humanities Research Center

Archer M. Huntington in Spain in 1892.

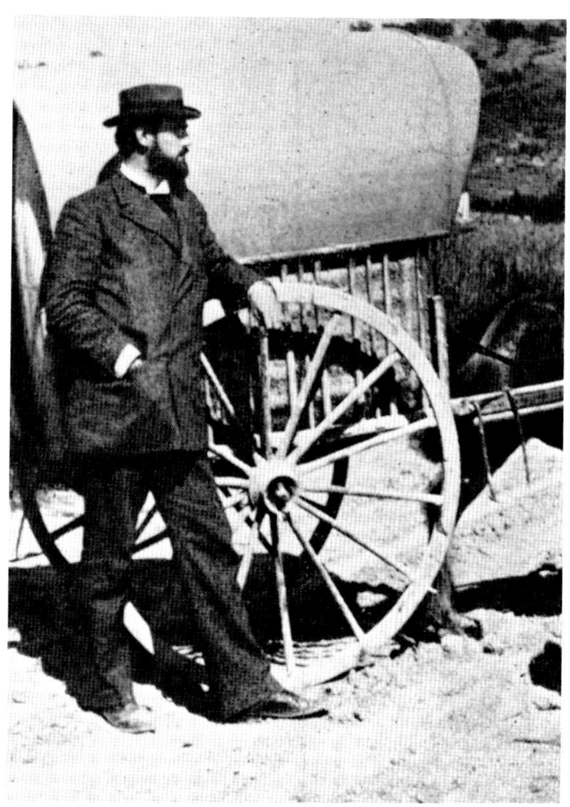

(now the Harry Ransom Center) opened, with two floors and storage devoted to the collections of the University Art Museum (now the Huntington Art Gallery). About that time Mr. and Mrs. John Duncan began to donate their important collection of contemporary Latin American art, making Texas the most important public collection of that material in the country. For years, Dr. Tom Cranfill of the English Department had been collecting Mexican prints and drawings, and he donated them to the University; Mr. M.K. Hage also donated much important Mexican art. The Latin American collection today contains more than 1400 works in all media. Mr. Harold Mertz's donation of his collection of Australian painting of the 1960s further broadened the scope of the collection.

Before 1980 museum purchases were few, but Dr. Goodall did obtain funding to increase both the Michener collection and the Latin American collection. In 1978 an advisory committee made up of Sherman Lee, Muriel Christison and Alan Shestack made recommendations for the future development of the art museum. The committee stressed that the collections on campus "should be immediately supplemented and then developed through acquisitions by purchase and gift of fine works in all areas of world art."[4] These recommendations were implemented by the new director, Dr. Eric McCready.

Since 1980 the American and Latin American collections have grown significantly, as has the collection of prints and drawings. In addition, new collection areas have been established and developed, most significantly ancient art and European painting.

A medieval collection was envisioned; so far it consists primarily of loans. With the ongoing exhibition of the permanent collection, the Huntington Art Gallery can now begin to represent the history of Western European and American art, providing primary sources for the study of art history, and cultural documents for all students, whether at the University or elsewhere.

Andrea S. Norris
Chief Curator

[1]Now in the Women's Dormitory Quadrangle
[2]Now exhibited in the Ransom Center galleries
[3]The following information is taken primarily from an excellent unpublished history of the University Art Museum by Dr. Marian B. Davis, who taught at The University and worked in the museum from 1944 to 1978
[4]Sherman E. Lee, "Summary Report on University of Texas Art Museum," 3 October 1978, 2.

NINETEENTH AND TWENTIETH CENTURY AMERICAN ART

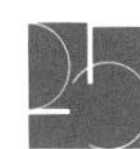

For at least twenty of the past twenty-five years, the Huntington Art Gallery has been actively building a superb teaching collection of twentieth century American painting. Begun with generous and long-term commitments from James and Mari Michener in the late 1960's, and re-commencing in 1983, the Michener Collection and the Huntington's twentieth century American collection is now considered the most unique, comprehensive, and finest on an American college campus today. In addition, another well-known collector, Mr. C. R. Smith, Washington, D.C., has made it possible for The University of Texas at Austin to house a major survey of nineteenth and twentieth century western American painting, an important complement to his collection of bronzes now at the Amon Carter Museum in Fort Worth.

Because of the depth of these two collections alone, a deliberate decision was reached to add to these strengths, and to continue focusing on periods of art history which interest students and professors alike, not only in the arts but also in many other academic disciplines. As mirrors of American culture, these paintings enable students to study history, literary trends, social and political mores, and a variety of other ethical and social concepts which have lead to extensive research, publication and new theoretical viewpoints.

Since 1983 when the Micheners again began actively supporting the Huntington's goals, 38 American paintings have been acquired for the permanent collection. In addition to the Michener Collection Acquisition Fund and the Archer M. Huntington Museum Fund, several new donors have stepped forward to help the Huntington enrich its contemporary holdings. They include: Mr. & Mrs. J. Neal Miller, Austin; Mr. & Mrs. Jack H. Herring, Austin; Mr. & Mrs. George Muellich, San Antonio; and, Ms. Patricia McHargue, Austin.

From the "New American Painting" exhibition, organized by the Director in 1984, a number of paintings were acquired with Michener and Huntington Funds. In all cases, the professional staff working with the donor studied the proposed works to insure that they were of such quality as to provide an intellectual base from which teaching could evolve and that the works were of the same high standard which existed for earlier acquisitions.

Occasionally staff members at the Museum are asked what is happening in American painting today. The general response has been, everything. Social and political commentary, historiography, portraiture, still life, abstraction, even the landscape—these have appeared or reappeared under various "isms" such as Neo-Expressionism and Neo-Geo. "Appropriation" has been a key word in the mid-1980's and one can only wonder where the concept of originality fits in today. Borrowing from the past—titles, styles, objects, even complete paintings themselves—these are all combined in the latest trend. The difficulties of being an original artist today, consistently striving for the "new" and the "innovative," are tempered by an art market expectant on the latest annual fad making it extremely difficult to be whatever "original" means especially to those who believe that the "new" must be pursued even at the expense of quality. The ideas behind painting seem to change as quickly as do the expected sizes of the canvas themselves: witness the large canvases of the earlier 1980's and the very small paintings being made today.

The 1980's has been a decade when it has been acceptable to paint "bad" paintings

James and Mari Michener in the Huntington Art Gallery in the Ransom Center, ca. 1970.

and find them marketable. Today this seems to be changing towards carefully crafted and more substantial art. Perhaps quality also is in transition. Future generations will have the task of deciding just how carefully and how well these paintings succeeded.

One of the most interesting aspects of the Huntington's collection of American painting is how well it has stood the test of time and, consequently, how substantial so many of the pictures seem in retrospect. In the late 1960's when several collections were given to The University of Texas, skepticism abounded. People in Austin were not aware of just how deeply abstract expression was influencing postwar movements and what transpired even before the war. With almost 30 and in some cases 50 years hindsight, many of these artists look better and better and lesser known names are becoming internationally recognized. One can only admire the wisdom of James and Mari Michener. The perception of these works by the general public has also been greatly enhanced thanks largely to public education, specifically a nationally recognized program of art education from K through 12 in the Austin Independent School District, throughout multiple schools and colleges of The University of Texas, and in the Austin and Central Texas communities.

Perhaps the greatest strength in the

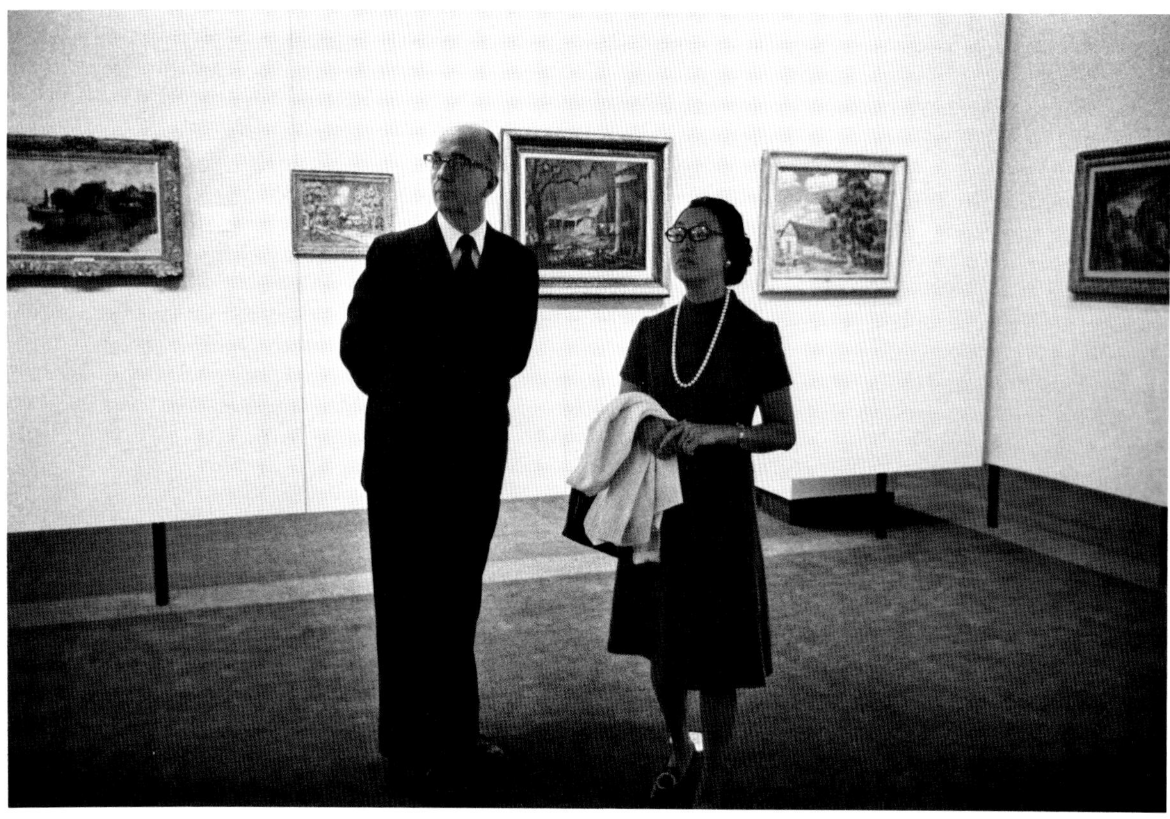

Huntington's twentieth century collections is that although they are comprehensive, with isolated examples by well recognized artists, greater depth exists with whole groups of work from a specific decade, school, or style. In turn, these bodies of paintings have become exhibitions themselves, ones which have been and will continue to be circulated nationally within the very near future.

While on the one hand major strengths exist, severe gaps remain of work by well-known artists like Rothko, Pollock, DeKooning, and Rosenquist to name only a few. Since the acquisition of major works by these internationally recognized painters is completely beyond the financial capabilities of the Huntington, it is hoped that donors will step forward to enrich the collection, which in turn will influence generations to come.

Not only do significant gaps remain in American painting, but the entire field of twentieth century sculpture is almost non-existent in the Huntington's permanent collections. Figuration and abstraction in all media could provide faculty with primary objects with which to teach. At present, our students suffer from this lack. Again, donors are badly needed to help the Huntington.

In summary, pioneering gifts of collections from the twentieth century to the Huntington have become its core, resulting in the addition of many other important pictures to these growing collections. Eventually, if a new building can ever be built, the wealth of materials within the Huntington's collection and from others around The University of Texas at Austin campus could be combined and shown as a significant, highly useful research center for the visual arts not only for Austin but for the United States as well.

Eric S. McCready
Director

AMERICAN PAINTING AND SCULPTURE

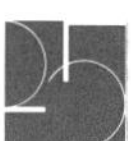

By definition, a museum is an institution devoted to the procurement, care, study, and display of objects of lasting interest or value, and a place where these objects are exhibited. The responsibilities implied in this definition are keenly felt by all who participate in the process of acquisition at the Huntington. Nowhere else in the gallery's collections has that mandate been more successfully met than in its collection of American paintings. Though the Huntington's youthful twenty-five years suggest an infant stage when compared to other collection programs of major museums in this country and abroad, our gallery is unusually fortunate to already have in place a broad survey of twentieth-century American painting and a substantial coverage of earlier periods of American art.

From its opening date in 1963, the Huntington (then known as the University Art Museum) has demonstrated its dedication to the exhibition and collection of paintings by American artists. The first paintings acquired by the gallery were a group of works by contemporary American artists given to the museum by the Longivew Foundation of New York. The gift was in recognition of the planned opening of the University's new museum space in 1963. The following year the museum received from Peter Neumann a painting by the twentieth-century American artist Carl Holty, and a painting and two sketches by the nineteenth-century American, Thomas Eakins, were donated by the artist's niece, Dr. Caroline Crowell.

Other acquisitions of works by American painters followed, but in so many ways, the most consequential addition to the collection has been the James and Mari Michener Collection of Twentieth-Century American Painting. From its inception, it has been a cornerstone on which the evolution of the museum's collections has been predicated. Providing both for aesthetic fulfillment and University scholarship, this extraordinary trust for future generations is the result of the outstanding benevolence of the Micheners. Dedicated to the preservation of America's aesthetic and cultural history, and steadfast in their support for the visual arts here at the University, the Micheners have given or helped the Gallery acquire a total of 375 paintings by twentieth-century artists, including 172 works on long-term loan.

Other donors have added importantly to the Huntington's American painting and sculpture collection. Outstanding among these is Mr. C. R. Smith of Washington, D.C., whose gifts (along with some long-term loans) to the Huntington of almost 100 American western paintings and sculpture have extended the range and perspective of the American collection, complimenting and expanding the coverage of American painting initiated by the Micheners. Though the C. R. Smith Collection of Western American Art is perhaps not as broad in its representation as is the Michener twentieth-century collection, the paintings and sculpture assembled by Mr. Smith form an important body of work which offers the basis for a serious program in the study of pre-modern art in America. Through his gifts of paintings dating from the early 1800s into the first half of the twentieth century, Mr. Smith has provided the Huntington with examples of landscape, genre, and historical painting traditions found in the pre-modern painting movements of this country. Together the Michener and Smith collections forge an historical and aesthetic continuum which provides the chronological framework needed for a serious program in the study of the history of American art.

1. GEORGE SEGAL, American, b. 1924-, *Blue Woman in Black Chair*, 1981, painted plaster, Archer M. Huntington Museum Fund, 1983.25.

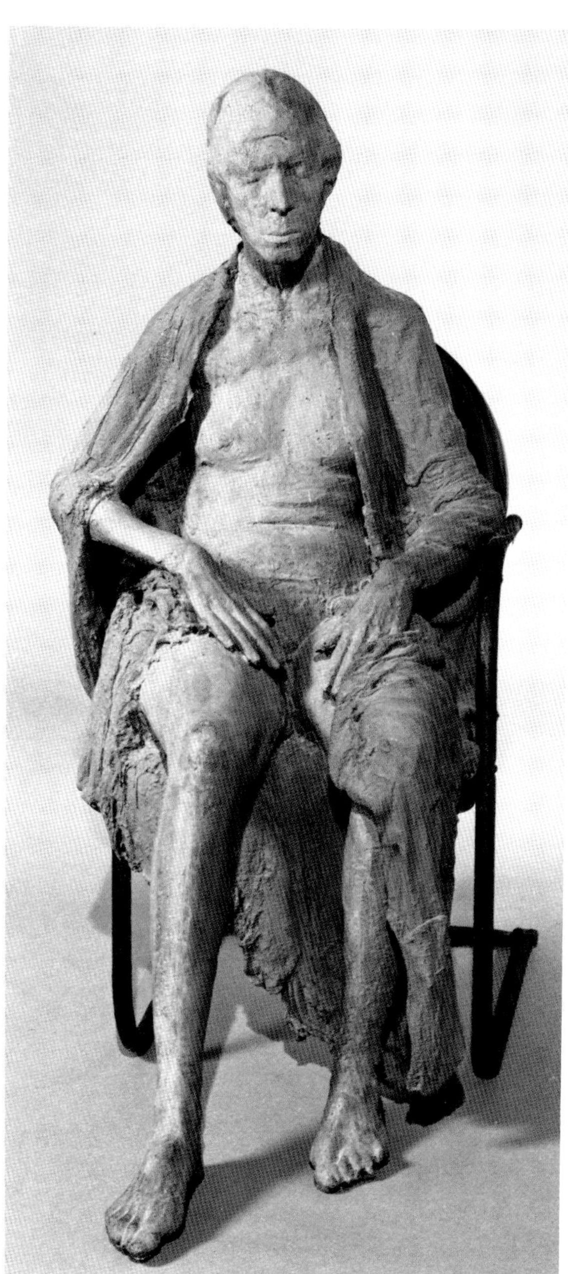

The significance of the American collection as a resource for scholarship has been instrumental in determining the academic five-year plan recommended in 1987 by the Dean of the College of Fine Arts. The plan proposed by the dean calls for the establishment of a chair for an internationally recognized scholar in art history, chosen to compliment the existing strengths of the program of art history in the department of art, and designed to rely on the support of the Huntington's American and Latin American collections. The dean's proposal has been translated into action by the art history program here at the University, resulting in the establishment of an endowed senior teaching position linked to the formation of a University Center for the Interdisciplinary Study of Modernism. The Center, which will serve as an impetus to the interdisciplinary study of modernism in art and related fields for graduate students and faculty alike, will draw on the scholarship potential of the Huntington's collection of American (and Latin American) art.

Over the years, the American painting collection has received numerous donations from institutions and individuals other than the Micheners and Mr. Smith, each serving to enrich the breadth and significance of the collection and to provide stimulus and foundation for future acquisitions. In addition to the gifts received from donors, the American collection has grown through purchases made by the Huntington, including paintings and sculpture from the eighteenth and early nineteenth centuries. More often than not in the contemporary area, even these purchases have been in various degrees underwritten by the Micheners. In a number of other cases, selections have been under the aegis of the director's discretionary funds, relying on the director's special expertise in the contemporary fields.

Regrettably, the acquisition of American sculpture by the Huntington has been very limited. Mr. Smith has given four sculpture pieces to the collection including works by Hugo Robus and Solon Borglum, and a Remington bronze was transferred to the collection from the University's library system. Acting to move beyond its very elementary sculpture holdings, the Huntington has purchased during the last five years the exhibition's seated figure by George Segal (fig. 1), and a corner piece by Carl Andre. Added to these has been Mary Callery's cast bronze work, *Acrobats*, a gift from Hester Diamond of New York.

There are, inevitably, many other voids in the American collection and the most basic list of desiderata will include works by a sizeable number of artists. Notable, for example, by their absence from the collection are works by such stellar twentieth-century figures as Jackson Pollock, Willem de Kooning, Frank Stella, and the late work of Mark Rothko. In turn, the nineteenth-century collection lacks adequate coverage of most of the important developments during that century, from the Hudson River school of landscape painting to the painting of the transcendentalists at the end of the century. In a period of acquisition limited to a bare generation, the Huntington has built an American collection of importance. Extreme diligence in scholarship and discovery will be required to meet the obligations encumbent upon the Gallery in the care and nurture of such a collection. We believe the Huntington will meet these challenges with continued success.

During the five years covered by this exhibition, the Huntington has added a total of 160 paintings to the American component. Of these, thirty-eight have been acquired as a result of Mr. and Mrs. Michener's direct gift or partial funding. Noteworthy among these is the painting (not in the exhibition) by Robert Jessup, *The Millstone*, an enigmatic and expressionist painting monumental in feel and style. The selection of the Jessup work is due to a collaboration in the acquisition process between the Micheners and the Huntington. Though in the work of Arch Connelly, the artist's sense of adventure and inventiveness offers a quite different aesthetic from *The Millstone*, the work of both artists closely connects with the stylistic developments of the 1980s. The Connelly provides an example of a work purchased under the director's discretionary fund.

The remainder of the American works in the exhibition also point to the collection's variety. Reflecting many of the contemporary trends in American painting the exhibition includes traditionally representative works by Miller (fig. 2) and Wilson (fig. 3), the realism of each work touched by the individual artist's private fantasies. Hovering between the recognizable and the obscure, the works by Kessler and Messer merge identifiable elements from the real world with the abstract, and in Kessler's instance, present a visual vocabulary reminiscent of the surrealists. In contrast, the work by Wolff is an example of abstraction and pattern apparently uninhabited by layered meanings such as those hidden in the Kessler and Messer works. Belonging to the neo-movements of the 1980s, the neo-expressionist sculpture by Bolt shares with the expressionist painting by Mason a figure whose anthropormorphic nature is made equivocal through the action of color and texture upon the image. The Bowman work is by an artist who once said there are no innocent bystanders. Its political comment

2. MELISSA MILLER, American, b. 1951-, *Zebras and Hyenas*, 1985, oil on linen canvas, Michener Collection Acquisition Fund, 1985.169.

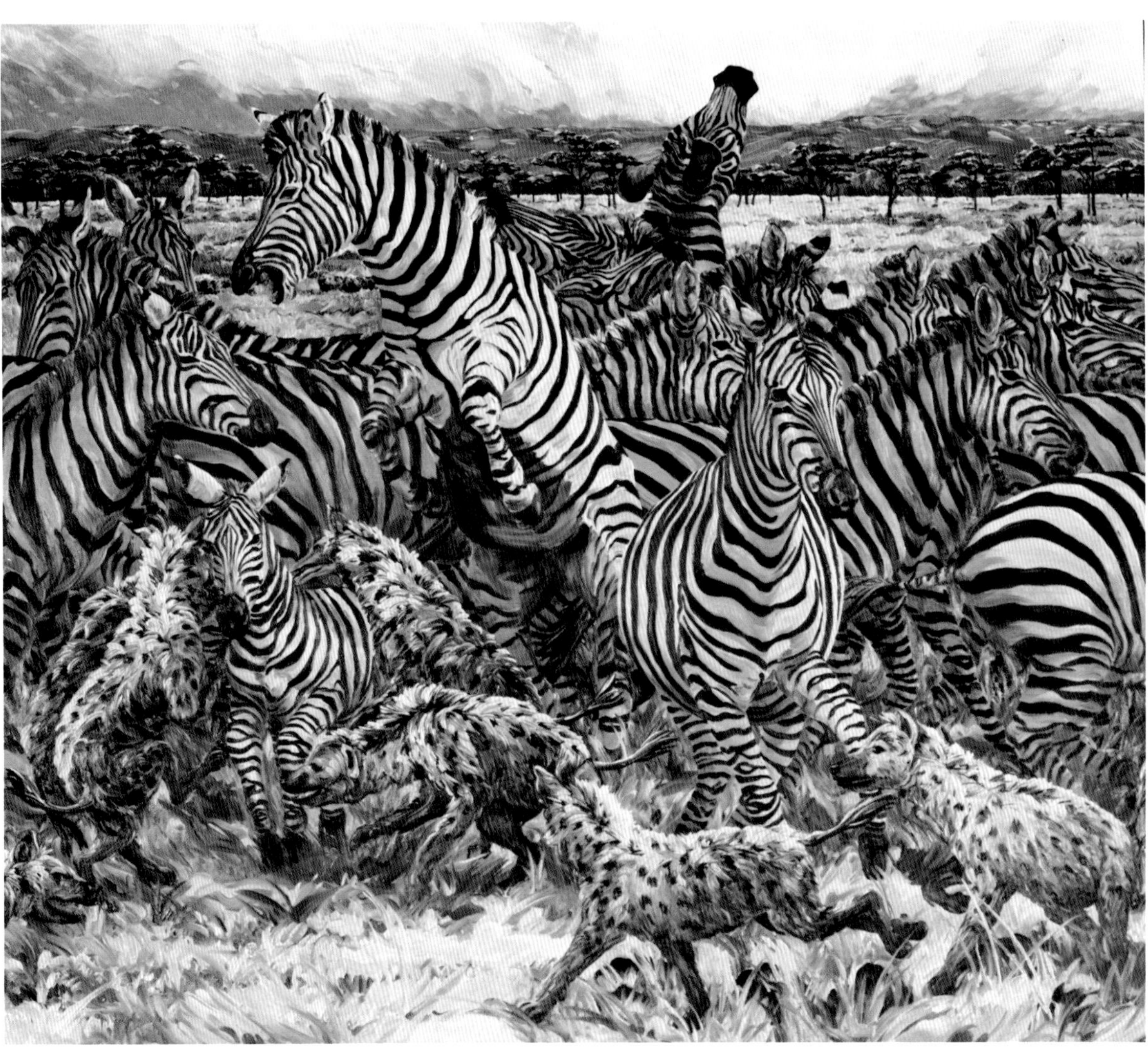

lies quietly under a highly individualized painting technique employing mass production printing techniques with metal powders added to the artist's pigments, all laid down on a Rubens-like crimson underpainting. Also dependent on an unusual technique, Slocum employs a turn of the century photo process to reveal his image. The Larmon (fig. 4) and the Nelson point to the trend today by some artists to work in a smaller format, and to make reference to the style of old master paintings, presenting these elements as excerpts from the past imposed upon a modern format. Finally, among the contemporary examples in the exhibition, the Falk demonstrates the interest currently held by some artists in drawing as painting, and suggests the artist's whimsy and wit, while the mood of the Todd is more elusive, incorporating the spell of the written word on its borders.

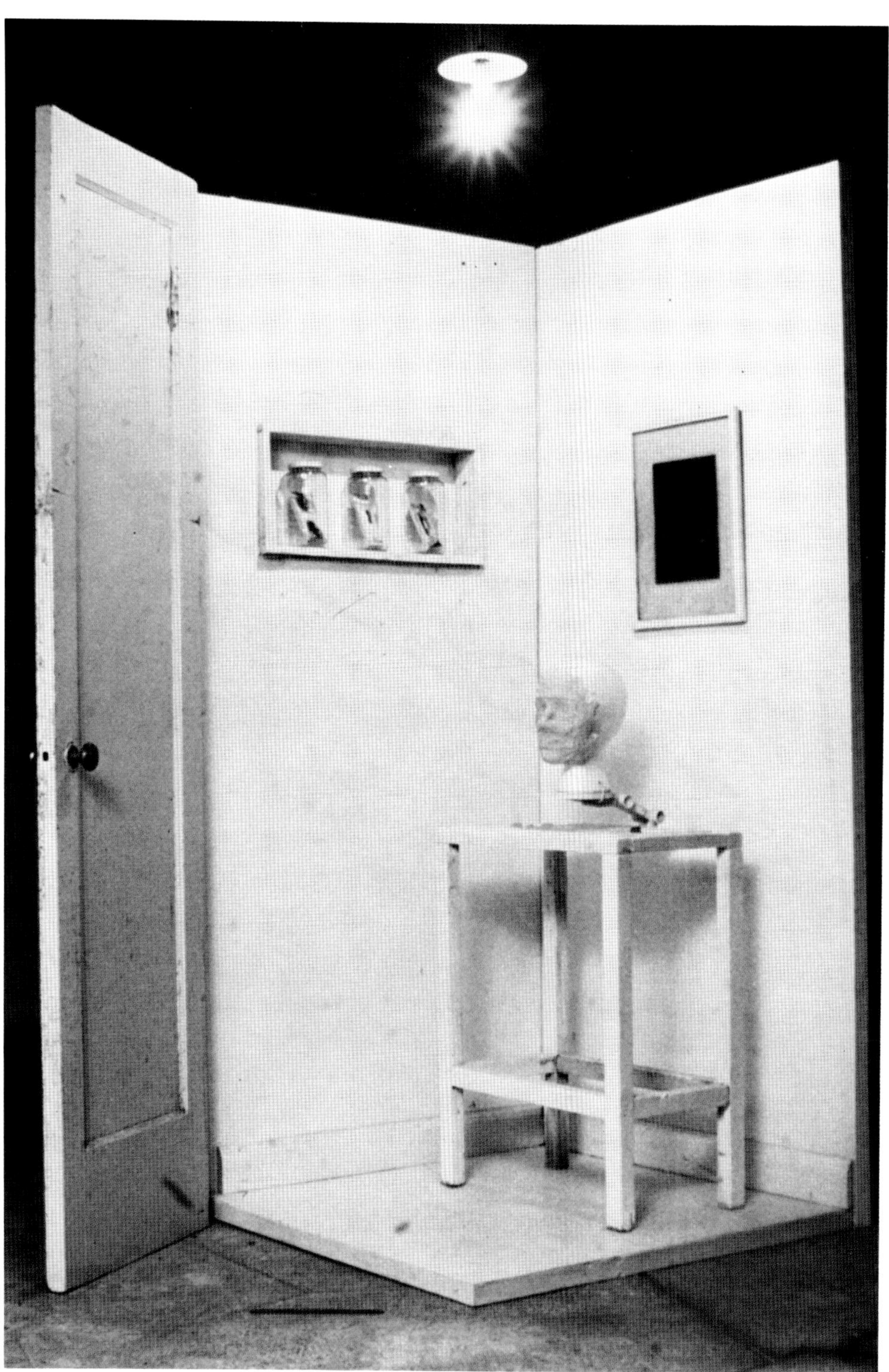

3. MARIA BRITO-AVELLANA, Cuban, b. 1947-, *The Conception*, 1983, wood and mixed media, gift of Ricardo Pau-Llosa, 1985.*22*.

4. JULIO LARRAZ, American, b. 1944-, *Casabas Under Cover*, 1979, oil on canvas, Barbara Duncan Fund, 1986.218.

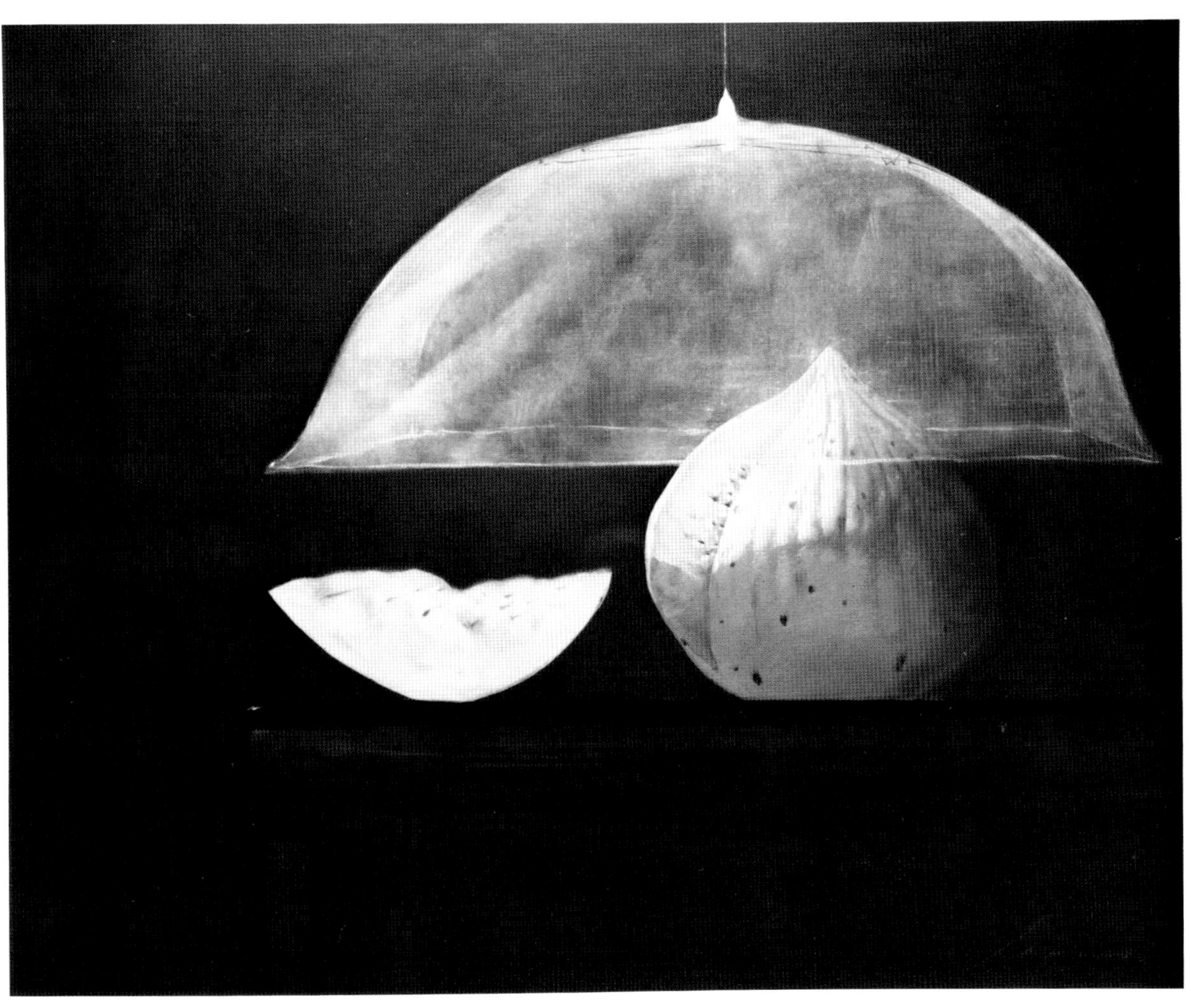

5. HUMBERTO CALZADA, Cuban, b. 1944-, *The Garden*, 1984, acrylic on canvas, gift of Ricardo Pau-Llosa, 1984.64.

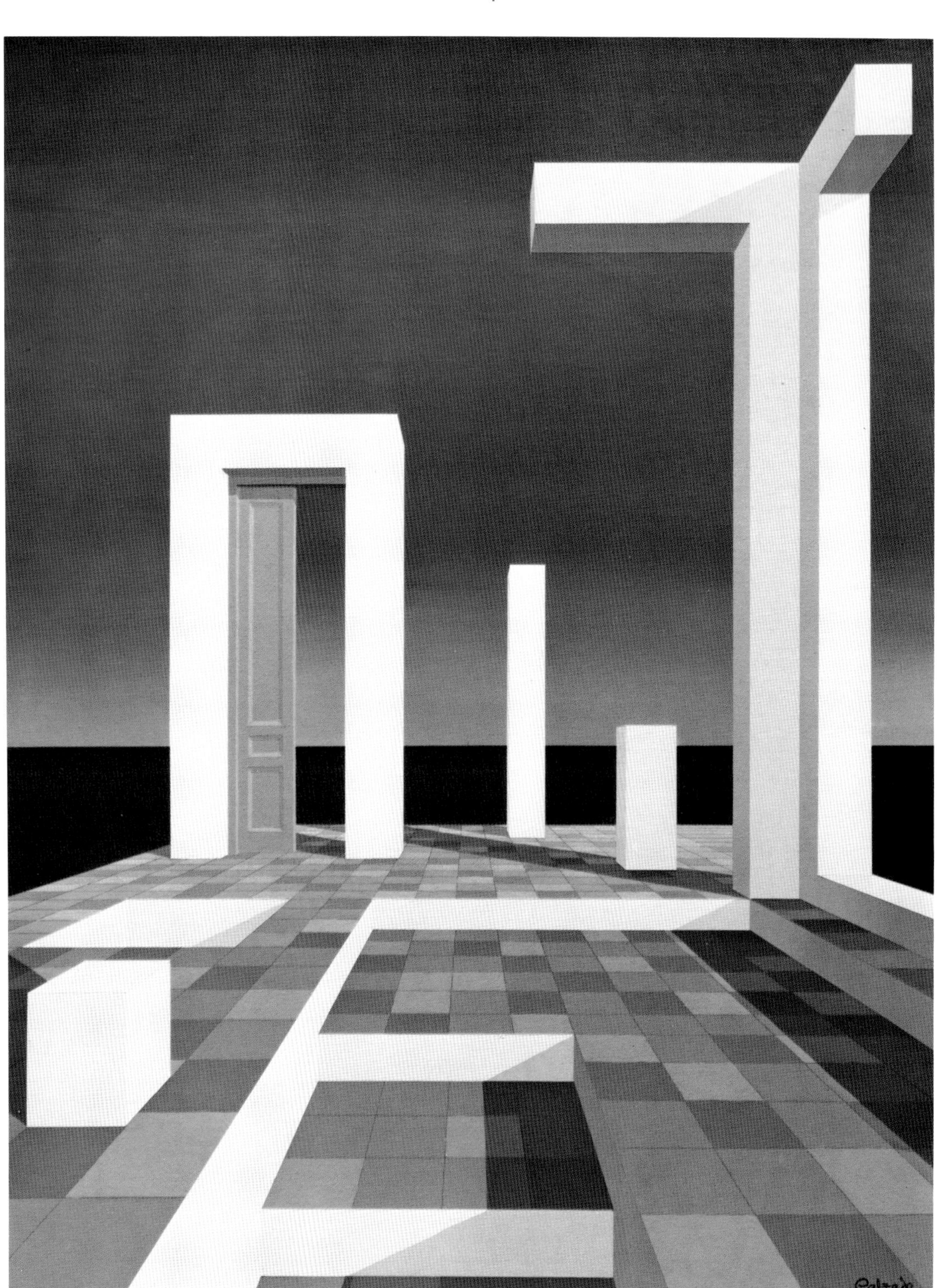

MARIA BRITO-AVELLANA
Cuban, 1947–
The Conception, 1983
Wood and mixed media
Gift of Ricardo Pau-Llosa, 1985.22

HUMBERTO CALZADA
Cuban, 1944–
The Garden, 1984
Acrylic on canvas
Gift of Ricardo Pau-Llosa, 1984.64

JUAN EGENAU
Chilean, 1927–
Caja enigmatica (Puzzle Box), 1982
Aluminum
Barbara Duncan Fund, 1985.65

MANUEL FELGUEREZ
Mexican, 1928–
Tres sectores circulares (Three Circular Sectors), n.d.
Painted metal (welded steel?)
Gift of Carol Straus, 1986.290

RAFAEL FERRER
Puerto Rican, 1933–
La isla pasa, 1978
Oil pastel on navigation map sewn behind plastic
Barbara Duncan Fund, 1984.75

GYULA KOSICE
Argentinian, b. Czechoslovakia, 1924–
Hydrolight, ca. 1975
Plexiglass, light, motor, and water in a wooden case
Gift of Barbara Duncan, 1986.304

JULIO LARRAZ
American, b. Cuba, 1944–
Casabas Under Cover, 1979
Oil on canvas
Barbara Duncan Fund, 1986.218

MARTA MINUJÍN
Argentinian, 1943–
Pauta transformacional, 1982
Plaster
Gift of Ricardo Pau-Llosa, 1986.111

GUSTAVO OJEDA
Cuban, 1958–
Four Lights, 1983
Oil on canvas
Archer M. Huntington Museum Fund, 1984.93

AUGUSTO TORRES
Uruguayan, b. Spain, 1913
Untitled, n.d.
Oil on jute canvas
Barbara Duncan Fund, 1985.31

PRINTS AND DRAWINGS

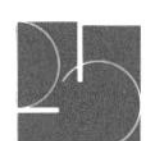

In the late twentieth century, as the supply of Old Master material dwindles, new areas of collecting become costly fads, and contemporary works provoke wild speculation, works of art on paper remain, in most cases, enticing possibilities. Prints and drawings are usually more available numerically, fine qualitatively, and affordable financially than any other class of object from a given culture or era. At the same time, they have come to be appreciated intellectually and academically as valid bases of historical interpretation in all but a few contexts and institutions (then identifiable as reactionary). No one would claim that a Mantegna school engraving (cover illustration) somehow equals a late canvas by the master, just that the former can be found more readily, acquired more reasonably, even speak as eloquently about the Italian Renaissance, the revival of Antiquity, the court of the Gonzaga, and Mantegna's historical place to listeners properly prepared.

It was an awareness of precisely these circumstances, of the art market and art history, that decided the priority of prints and drawings at the Huntington from the time of its reorganization in 1979–80. In what other realm could an ambitious, fast-growing, and research-oriented museum accumulate more, of higher quality and greater interest, at less expense? The present exhibition confirms the wisdom of that decision, as it recalls some of the most conspicuous successes from the first phase of what became a program for collecting works of art on paper. At the same time, especially with a representative group of major purchases from the past year, it heralds a second phase of even deeper commitment. The Huntington is one of only two university museums so assiduously pursuing this area, and can already be said to possess the finest, most balanced group of prints in the South. Both that status and reputation seem destined to grow.

The collecting of works of art on paper has always posed a special challenge. From the sixteenth century and Aretino's desperation for the slightest sketch by Michelangelo as a spark of genius captured, drawings have been perceived as the least mediated, but also least easily quantified, form of visual expression. From the next century and Pierre-Jean Mariette's commissions to assemble comprehensive collections of engravings and etchings, prints have been recognized as a well-mapped but vast terrain, requiring long experience and sure footing to traverse. In a sense, then, opposite challenges: one, a translation from a particular as variable and intangible as personality itself to a more stable generic; the other, from a sure structure to a minutely inflected incidental. But, more essentially, the connoisseurship of prints and drawings proceeds identically, based upon constant induction, long retention, and sympathetic abstraction of visual data in a process that, at its best, comes to resemble intuition.

While time, new means of visual documentation, and the systematic gains of modern scholarship have somewhat diminished this fundamental cognitive challenge, a program such as the Huntington's introduces another serious question, of strategy. Simply, since there are so many possibilities, yet resources are not without limit, what are to be the focuses of collecting? How are fortunate choices to be made? Here, "The Huntington at 25" should prove most instructive. Every work on paper evinces both aesthetic discrimination, calculated allocation, and responsibility to a number of publics. The acquisition of a particularly fine impression of masterpiece by Rembrandt in a relatively common state

1. REMBRANDT VAN RIJN, Dutch, 1606–1669, *Clement De Jonghe, Printseller*, 1651, etching, drypoint and burin, v/vi, Archer M. Huntington Museum Fund, 1987.87.

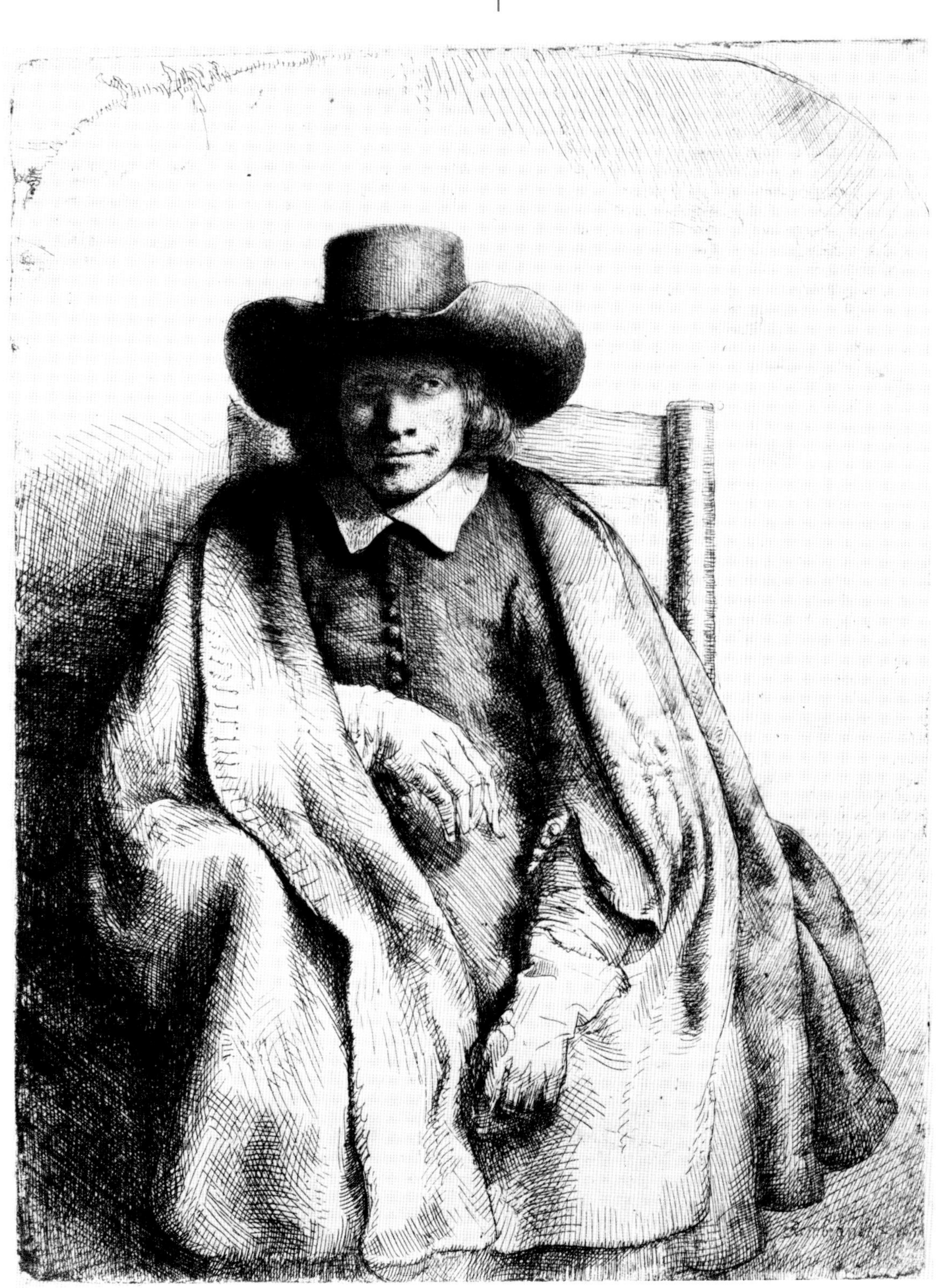

2. DIEGO RIVERA, Mexican, 1886–1957, *Nude, Frida Kahlo*, 1930, lithograph, unnumbered proof, Archer M. Huntington Museum Fund, 1986.103.

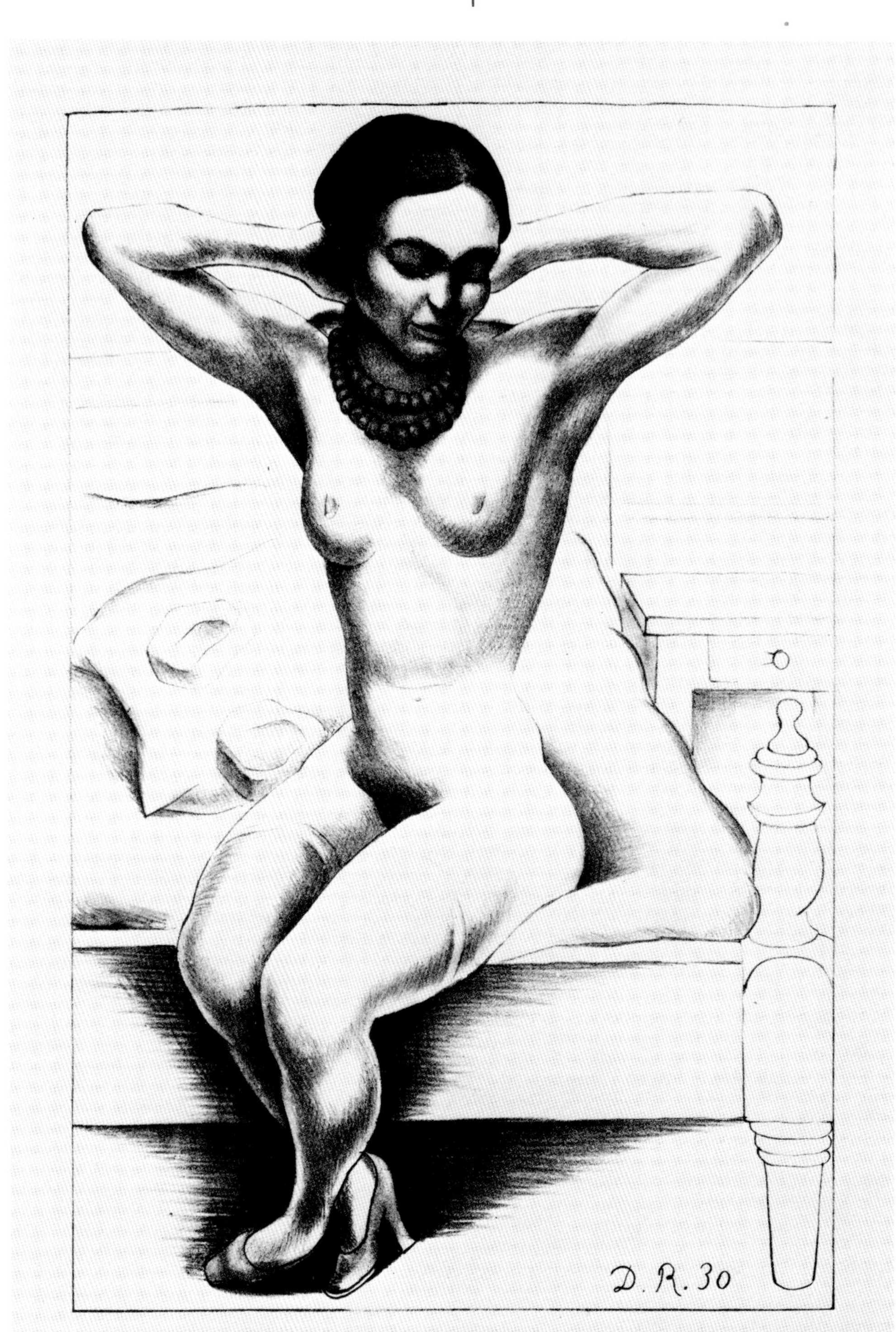

3. WIFREDO LAM, Cuban, 1902–1982, *Sin Titulo (Untitled)*, 1957, charcoal and pencil, Archer M. Huntington Museum Fund, 1986.58.

(fig. 1) reflects much more than the connoisseurship and personal tastes of a curator and accessions committee. It depends upon a knowledge of monetary worth, other impressions available, other Rembrandts already in the collection, the probability, or not, of subsequent acquisitions of the kind, and the usefulness, compared to other prints by Rembrandt or merely at such expense, to undergraduates exploring seventeenth-century Holland, printmakers studying intaglio technique, and visitors wishing to see "something great."

What are the more general principles, the strategy of collecting, made evident by the works on paper in this exhibition? First, and not circularly, reinforcing existing strengths. Given the Gallery's renown as a repository of Latin American art, the purchase of a significant group of modern Mexican works, with no less than seven Rivera drawings and some two dozen lithographs (fig. 2), as well as a superb Lam (fig. 3) from the critical year of 1957, supplies a vital and previously missing chapter. The same logic determines the acquisition of contemporary

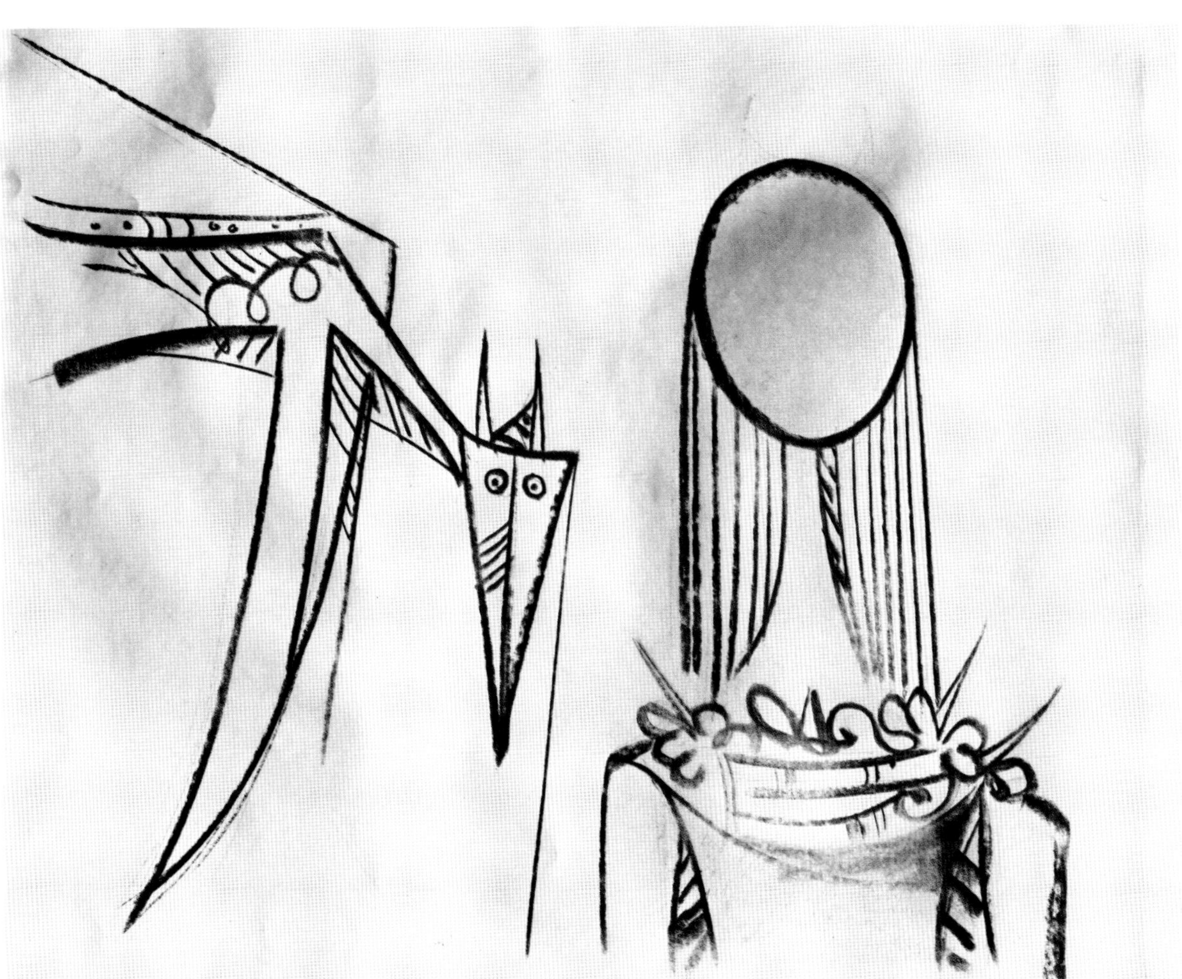

4. LUIS CABALLERO, Colombian, 1943–, *Untitled*, 1985, charcoal on paper, Archer M. Huntington Museum Fund, 1986.2.

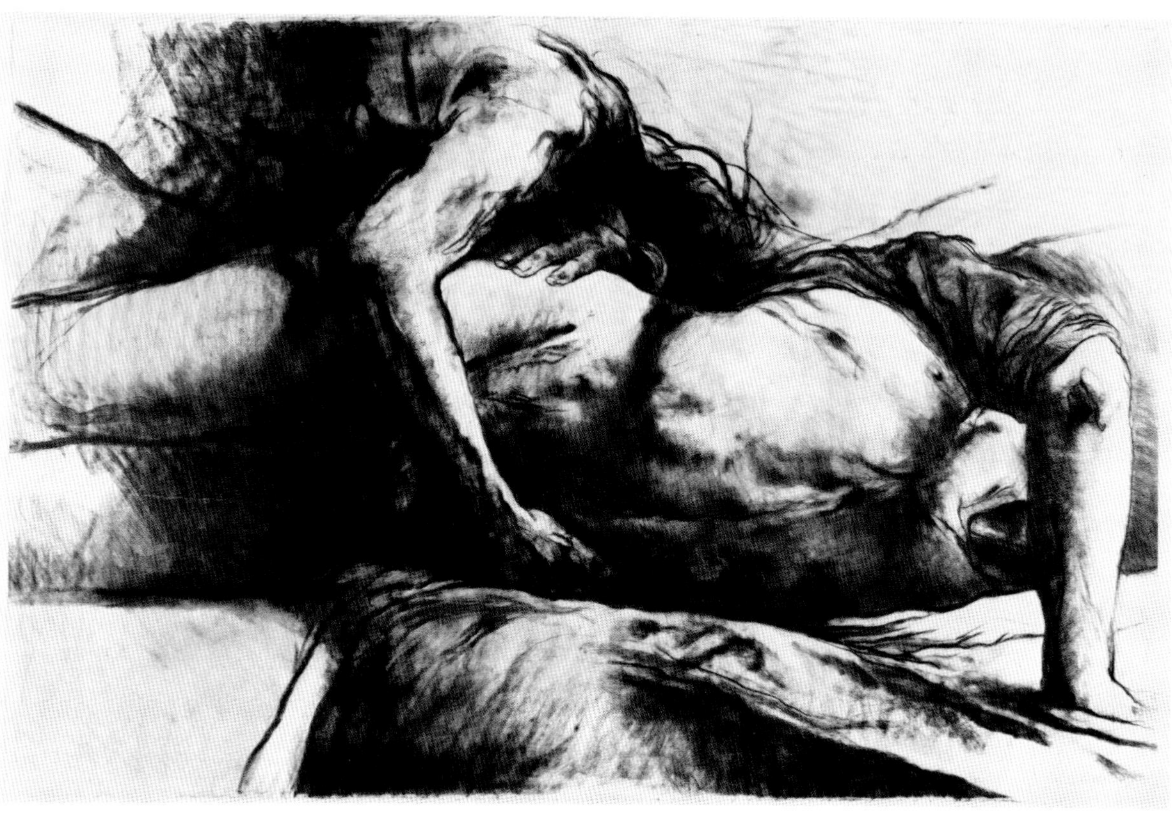

Latin works across a spectrum from the grand, tortured Caballero (fig. 4) to the cool, elegant Cugat. And the same is true of contemporary American art, anchored at the Huntington by the Michener Collector and by now nurtured over two decades. It is often carried forward with works on paper where little hope exists of an equivalent painting—Diebenkorn, Fischl, Murray, Sultan, Rauschenberg's sublime *Treaty* (fig. 5),—experiment with significant newer talent can be undertaken swiftly—the wonderfully varied group of App, Avery, Letscher,—or foreign trends of global reach can be conveniently documented—Beuys, Clemente. If the one strength follows from geography and an aspect of the region's culture, the other arises within the university and a studio art program so healthy that it even contributes directly to the Huntington's growth: works left by such recent Guest Artists in Printmaking as Wilson (fig. 6) and Surls are among the most important—and, with their accompanying proofs, unique—contemporary works in its possession.

Indeed, in a few special or even unexpected instances, a specific new strength, even a scholarly resource, may be determined by a major gift. This principle, of encouraging donations, may entail a curator and director's active pursuit, but in the best cases involves only their convincing a prospective

5. ROBERT RAUSCHENBERG, American, b. 1925–, *Treaty*, 1974, Color lithograph on two sheets, 12/31, Archer M. Huntington Museum Fund, 1987.85.

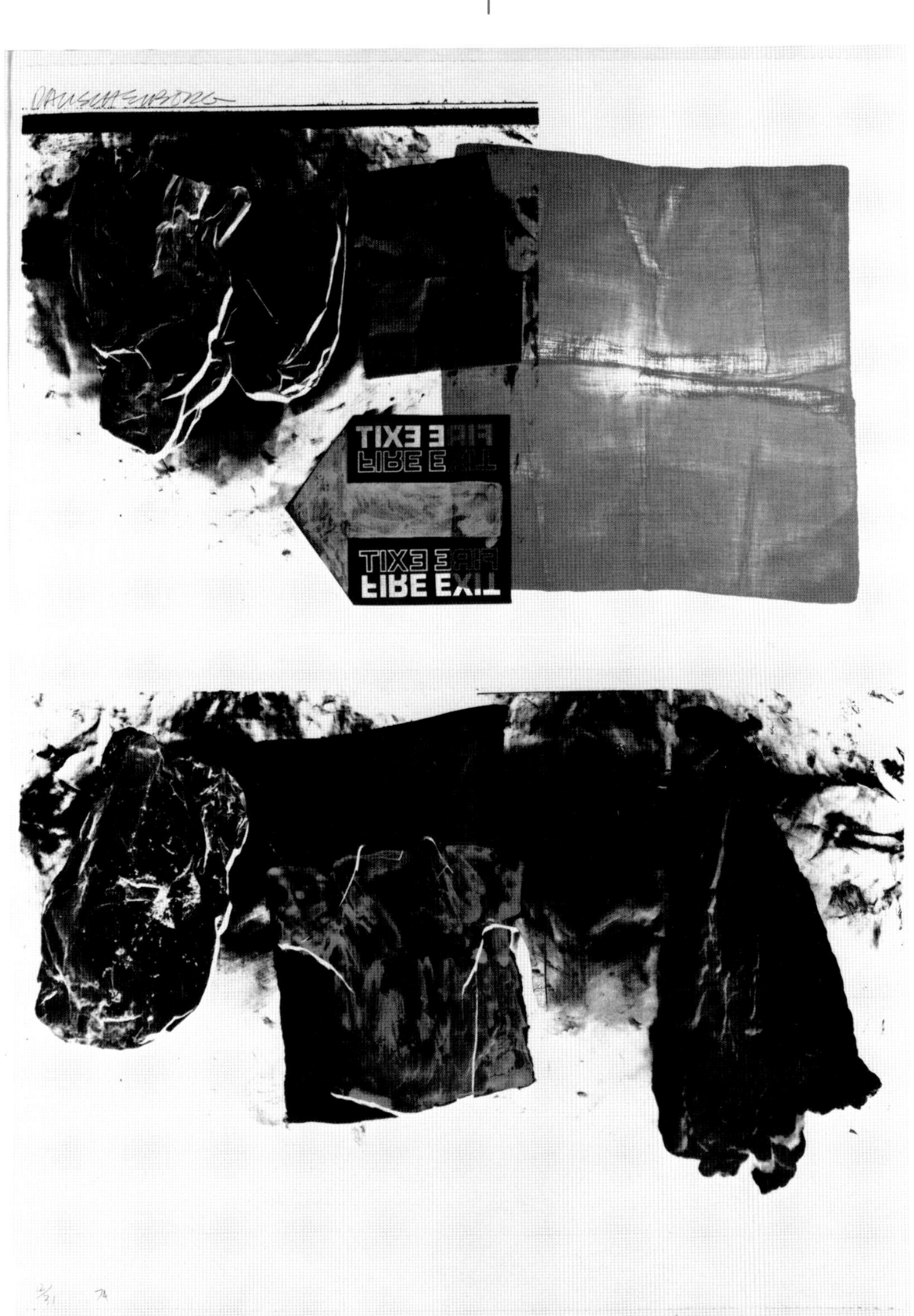

6. ROBERT WILSON, American, b. 1941–, *"Alceste", Act II SC.1*, 1986, lithograph, 20/20, Transfer from the Guest Artists in Printmaking Program, Art Department, The University of Texas at Austin, 1986.145.

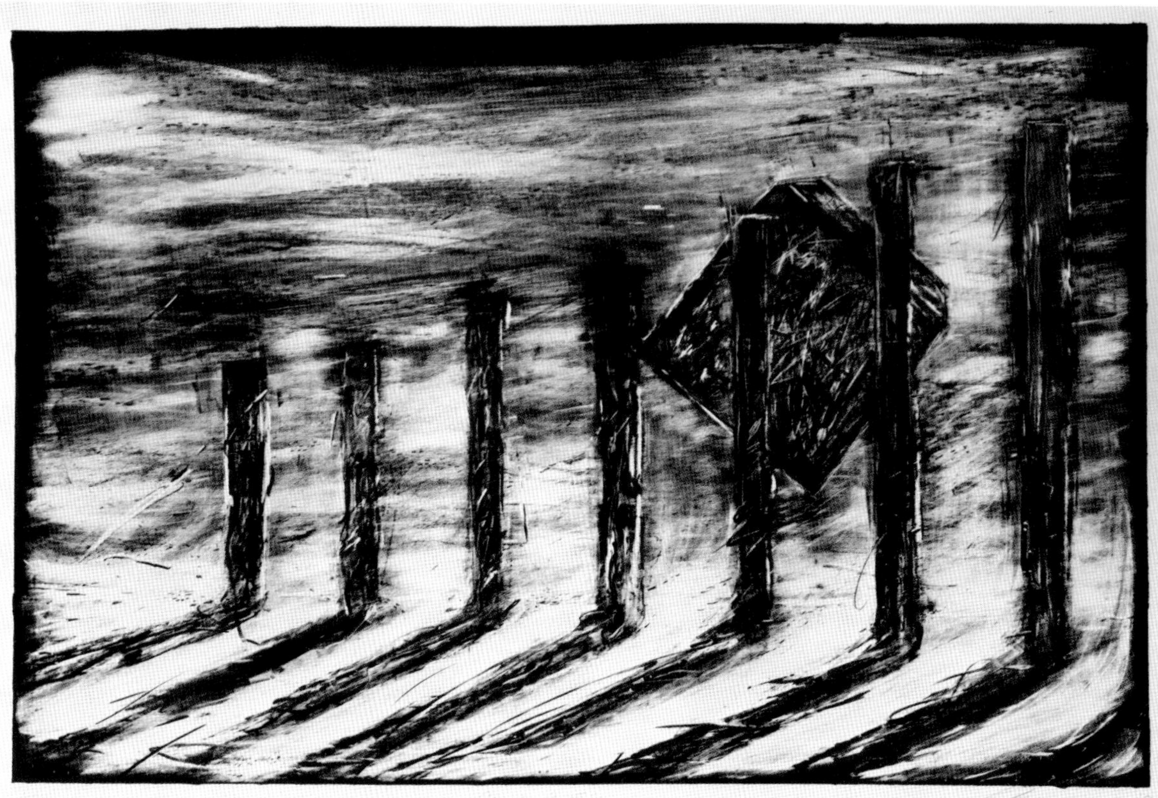

donor of the institution's virtues and the appropriateness of the contribution. Really, then, this wholesale addition of new dimensions to the collection depends much less on any strategy than on sheer generosity, over the past four years of such friends as Dr. & Mrs. Kenneth Prescott, Dr. and Mrs. Ira Jackson, Mrs. Karen Gutmann, and, through the Still Water Foundation, Mr. & Mrs. Stephen Wilkinson. Its results, in the acquisition of a nearly a dozen drawings by Burgoyne Diller (fig. 7), a fine group of hand-colored Gavarnis, sixteen drawings as well as several prints by the German "pre-Expressionist" Corinth, and virtually the complete graphic *oeuvre* of Clare Leighton (the largest single gift ever to the Gallery; fig. 8), are extraordinarily welcome both in themselves and as material befitting a research facility at a center of higher education.

In no area of collecting, however, must the strategy be more clear, the logic more precise, than in Old Master prints and drawings. Here, the alternatives in other media are fewest, the Gallery's holdings thinnest, the costs highest, yet the demand, of a faculty and community primarily concerned with the Western European tradition, greatest. It is obviously not enough that an impression be superb or a study handsome. Each work on

7. BURGOYNE DILLER, American, 1906–1965, *Untitled #38*, ca. 1936, pen and ink with colored washes, gift of Kenneth and Emma-Stina Prescott, 1985.179.

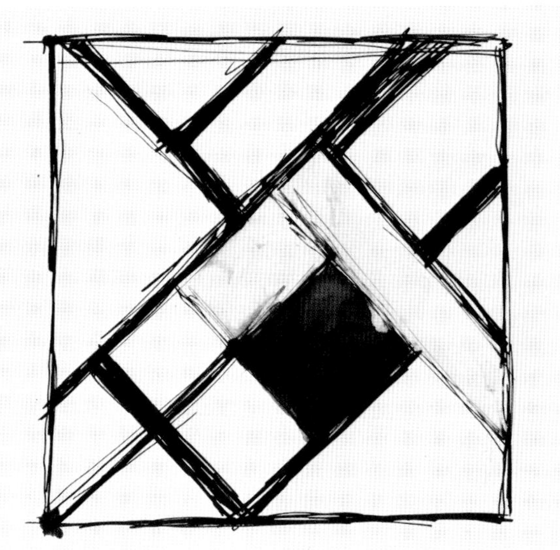

paper should also exemplify a technique, present an interesting subject, and assume a characteristic form, so that, at the very least, an artist, better, his culture, or, best, a period is typified. If reduced to a third principle it might be termed overdetermined choosing. Thus, Dürer's *Ravisher* (fig. 9) was selected because an early engraving generally, an early work by a singular master specifically, still medieval in subject, but already curiously individualized in rendition. The Agostino Veneziano is a rare, properly gray-toned impression of an early reproductive engraving, as close to the hand and mind of Raphael, and therefore to the classical tradition at its origins, as the Gallery can possess. The Ghisi is at once a superb Mannerist engraving and a favorite Renaissance allegory *all'antica*. Gratefully owed to the continuing involvement of Mr. Marvin Vexler, the De Launays (figs. 10, 11) reveal both the process of intaglio printing and the lightly moralizing cheer current in pre-Revolution France. The Earlom, along with five other mezzotints purchased in 1986, typify a technique and a genre basic to eighteenth-century English art. Attractive enough individually, the Baciccio (fig. 12) and the Granet (fig. 13) also illustrate extreme possibilities of certain media—the blushing lilt of red chalk, the disembodied luminosity of pen and wash—as they evoke nothing less than the tenor of two ages, the late Baroque and the Romantic.

These thumbnail accounts could, of course, be extended to considerable length, or offered for every Old Master work acquired over the past four years. The point, however, is clear, and should be underscored as the visitor to "The Huntington at 25" considers unnamed recent acquisitions. Each represents a choice, never casual, nor limited to a judgement of quality, rather, guided by a sense of the collection's balance, the Gallery's missions, and an opportunity to be seized before it too, within a generation, fades.

Jonathan Bober
Curator of Prints and Drawings

8. CLARE LEIGHTON, American, b. England, 1901, *Haymaking*, 1931, from *The Farmer's Year*, (London, 1933), wood engraving, proof, i/xx, gift of the Still Water Foundation, 1987.

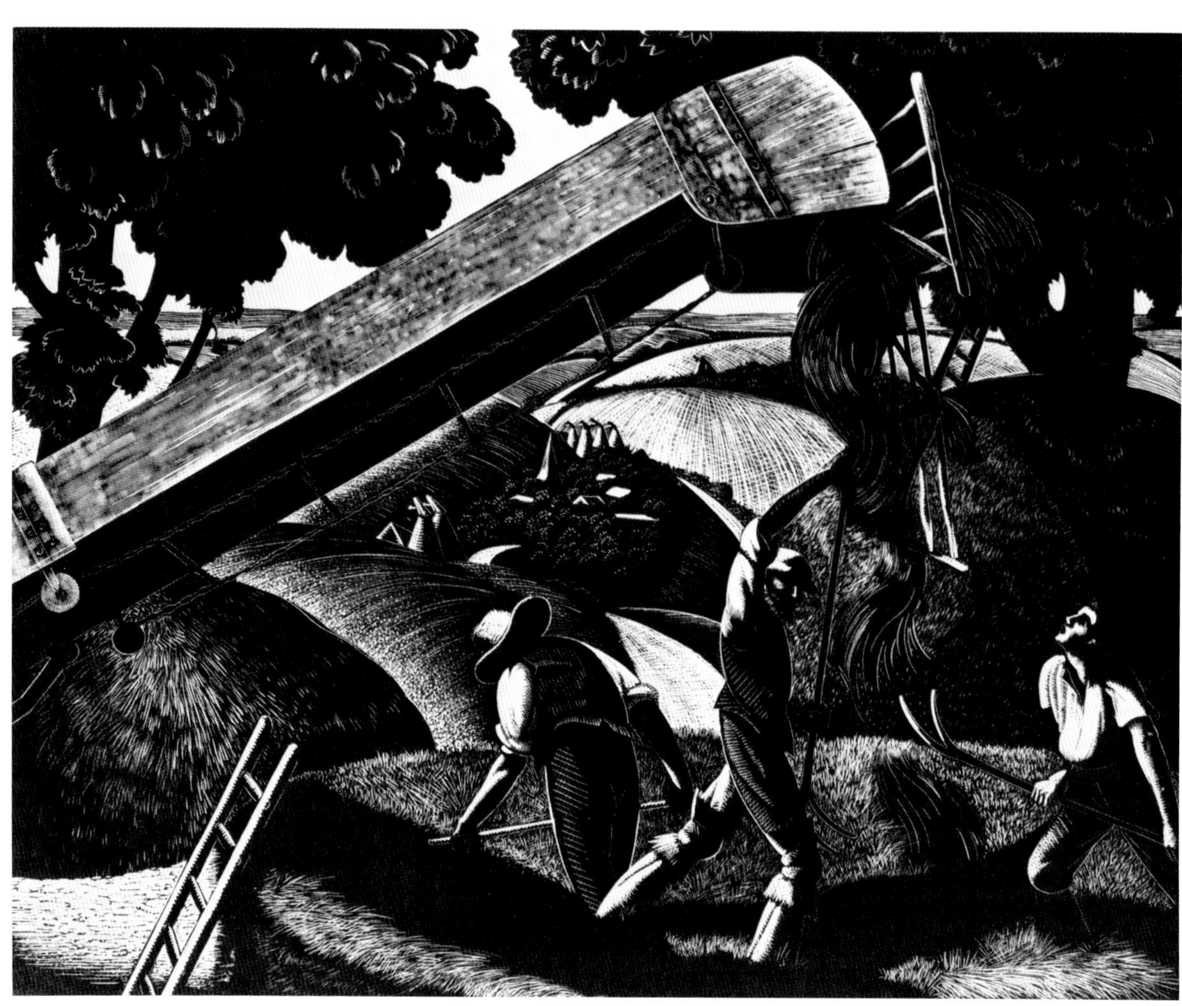

JORGE ALVARO
Argentinian, 1949–
La hora del te (*Tea Time*), 1982
Watercolor, charcoal and pencil
Archer M. Huntington Museum Fund, 1986.64

ANONYMOUS
Flemish, 15th C.
The Betrayal, from the *Leven Christi* (*Life of Christ*), 1488
Hand-colored woodcut
Archer M. Huntington Museum Fund, 1983.132.44/55

ANONYMOUS
German, 15th C.
St. Luke, the Evangelist, from the Tenth German Bible, 1485
Hand-colored woodcut
Archer M. Huntington Museum Fund, 1983.132.31/55

ANONYMOUS
Italian, 15th C.
Hypnerotomachia Poliphili (*The Dream of Poliphilus*), 1499
Woodcut
Archer M. Huntington Museum Fund, 1983.132.52/55

TIMOTHY APP
American, 1947–
Untitled I, 1986
Ink and acrylic on paper
Archer M. Huntington Museum Fund, 1987.89

ERIC AVERY
American, 1948–
False Bacchus, 1985
Photo-lithograph, nine-color screenprint, one-color linoleum cut, collage and hand gilding, 4/27
Archer M. Huntington Museum Fund, 1986.40

LARRY BELL
American, 1939–
Untitled, 1985
"Vapor drawing" (vaporized quartz on paper)
Archer M. Huntington Museum Fund, 1987.86

JOSPEH BEUYS
German, 1921–1986
Fünf Lithographien (*Five Lithographs*), 1977
Color lithograph, 28/60
Archer M. Huntington Museum Fund, 1987.82.1–5

LUÍS CABALLERO
Colombian, 1943–
Untitled, 1985
Charcoal on paper
Archer M. Huntington Museum Fund, 1986.2

FRANCESCO CLEMENTE
Italian, 1952–
Untitled B, 1986
Color lithograph on three sheets, 43/100
Archer M. Huntington Museum Fund, 1987.3

LOVIS CORINTH
German, 1858–1925
Double Portrait of Self with Dr. Karl Schwarz, 1916
Drypoint, unnumbered proof
Gift of Mrs. Karen Gutmann, 1987

LOVIS CORINTH
German, 1858–1925
Study of a Reclining Female Nude, 1904
Black chalk (double-sided)
Gift of Mrs. Karen Gutmann, 1987

DELIA CUGAT
Argentinian, 1930–
La Vispera (*Vespers*), 1985
Watercolor over pencil on paper
Archer M. Huntington Museum Fund, 1985.75

PHILIBERT-LOUIS DEBUCOURT
French, 1755–1832
Annette et Lubin, ca. 1785–90
Color aquatint, iii/v
Archer M. Huntington Museum Fund, 1985.9

RICHARD DIEBENKORN
American, 1922–
Ochre, 1983
Twelve-color, nineteen-block woodcut, 57/200
Purchased as a Gift of Marvin Vexler, Class of '48, 1984.42

BURGOYNE DILLER
American, 1906–1965
Untitled, ca. 1936
Black ink with blue, orange, yellow and black pastel
Gift of Kenneth and Emma-Stina Prescott, 1984.118

BURGOYNE DILLER
American, 1906–1965
Untitled #38, ca. 1936
Pen and ink with colored washes
Gift of Kenneth and Emma-Stina Prescott, 1985.179

BURGOYNE DILLER
American, 1906–1965
Untitled #78, ca. 1950
Pen and black ink with pencil
Gift of Kenneth and Emma-Stina Prescott, 1987.104

ALBRECHT DÜRER
German, 1471–1528
The Ravisher, ca. 1495
Engraving, Meder 76b
Archer M. Huntington Museum Fund, 1987.13

RICHARD EARLOM
English, 1743–1822
The Porter and the Hare, after Johann Joseph Zoffany, 1774
Mezzotint
Archer M. Huntington Museum Fund, 1985.7

ERIC FISCHL
American, 1948–
Untitled (Woman with Dalmation), 1987
Etching and aquatint, 74/100
Archer M. Huntington Museum Fund, 1987.103

JEAN-LOUIS FORAIN
French, 1852–1931
The Family, n.d.
Charcoal with stumping on buff paper
Gift of Latané Temple, 1985.97

GIOVANNI BATTISTA GAULLI,
called BACICCIO
Italian, 1639–1709
Study of a Woman's Head and Hands, ca. 1675–80
Red chalk on beige paper
Friends of the Archer M. Huntington
Art Gallery Purchase, 1987.16

GUILLAUME-SULPICE CHEVALIER
called PAUL GAVARNI
French, 1804–1866
L'homme à la cigarette, (self-portrait), 1842
Lithograph
Archer M. Huntington Museum Fund, 1986.5

GUILLAUME-SULPICE CHEVALIER,
called PAUL GAVARNI
French, 1804–1866
Les enfants terribles, no. 35, 1840–41
Hand-colored lithograph
Gift of Ira and Virginia Jackson, 1986.121

SULPICE-GUILLAUME CHEVALIER,
called PAUL GAVARNI
French, 1804–1866
Les enfants terribles, no. 36, 1840–41
Hand-colored lithograph
Gift of Ira and Virginia Jackson, 1986.122

GIORGIO GHISI
Italian, 1520–1582
The Calumny of Apelles, after Luca Penni, ca. 1560
Engraving, iii/v
Archer M. Huntington Museum Fund, 1987.49

GIOVANNI ANTONIO DA BRESCIA
Italian, active ca. 1490-after 1525
The Triumph of Caesar: The Elephants, after Mantegna, ca. 1490–95
Engraving
Archer M. Huntington Museum Fund, 1987.47

FRANÇOIS-MARIUS GRANET
French, 1775–1849
Monks Entering a Cloister, ca. 1802–19
Pen and brown ink with brown and grey washes on off-white paper
Archer M. Huntington Museum Fund, 1987.18

SAMUEL HIERONYMOUS GRIMM
Swiss, active in England, 1733–1794
Village by a River, France, 1768
Pen and ink and watercolor on paper
Archer M. Huntington Museum Fund, 1987.41

CARL-WILHELM KOLBE
German, 1757–1835
Cow amidst Vegetation, n.d.
Etching
Archer M. Huntington Museum Fund, 1987.88

ROBERT KUSHNER
American, 1949–
Water Bearer #26, 1987
Etching on handmade paper with gold appliqué, glitter and paint
Archer M. Huntington Museum Fund, 1988.1

WIFREDO LAM
Cuban, 1902–1982
Sin Título (*Untitled*), 1957
Charcoal and pencil
Archer M. Huntington Museum Fund, 1986.58

NICOLAS DE LAUNAY
French, 1739–1792
Le carquois epuisé (*The Empty Quiver*), after Pierre-Antoine Baudouin, 1765
Etching, 1st state
Purchased as a Gift of Marvin Vexler, Class of '48, 1985.86

9. ALBRECHT DÜRER, German, 1471–1528, *The Ravisher*, ca. 1495, engraving, Meder 76b, Archer M. Huntington Museum Fund, 1987.13.

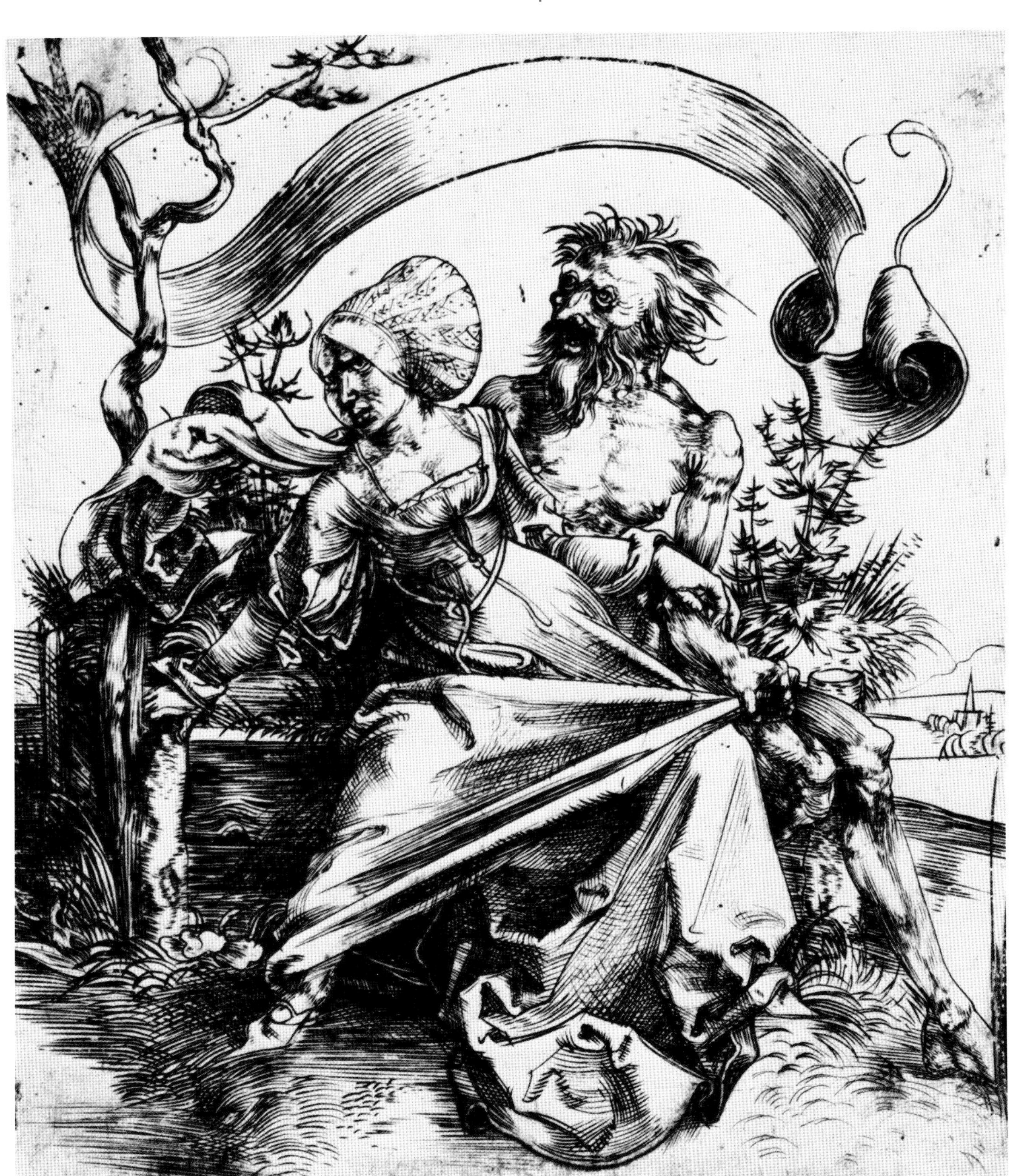

10. NICOLAS DE LAUNAY,
French, 1739–1792, *Le carquois epuisé* (*The Empty Quiver*), after Pierre-Antoine Baudouin, 1765, etching 1st state, purchased as a gift of Marvin Vexler, Class of '48, 1985.86.

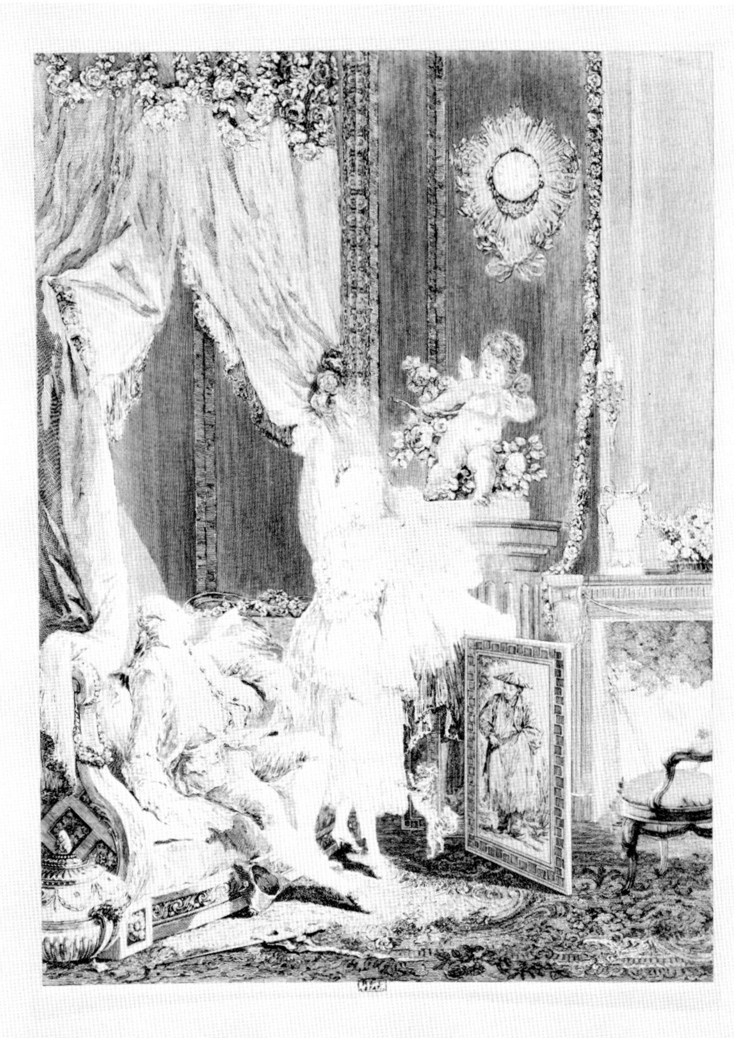

NICOLAS DE LAUNAY
French, 1739–1792
Le carquois epuisé (The Empty Quiver),
after Pierre-Antoine Baudouin, 1775
Etching and engraving, state before lettering
Purchased as a Gift of Marvin Vexler, Class of '48, 1985.87

CLARE LEIGHTON
American, b. England, 1901
Snow Shovellers, 1929,
from *The Legion Book*
(London, 1929)
Wood engraving, i/ii, 31/50
Gift of the Still Water Foundation, 1987

CLARE LEIGHTON
American, b. England, 1901
Haymaking, 1931,
from *The Farmer's Year*
(London, 1933)
Wood engraving, proof, i/xx
Gift of the Still Waer Foundation, 1987

CLARE LEIGHTON
American, b. England, 1901
The Fat Stock Market, 1932,
from *The Farmer's Year*
(London, 1933)
Wood engraving, proof
Gift of the Still Water Foundation, 1987

CLARE LEIGHTON
American, b. England, 1901
Berries, 1934,
from *Four Hedges*
(New York, 1935)
Wood engraving, 2/30
Gift of the Still Water Foundation, 1987

11. NICOLAS DE LAUNAY, French, 1739–1792, *Le carquois epiusé* (*The Empty Quiver*), after Pierre-Antoine Baudouin, 1775, etching and engraving, state before lettering, purchased as a gift of Marvin Vexler, Class of '48, 1985.87.

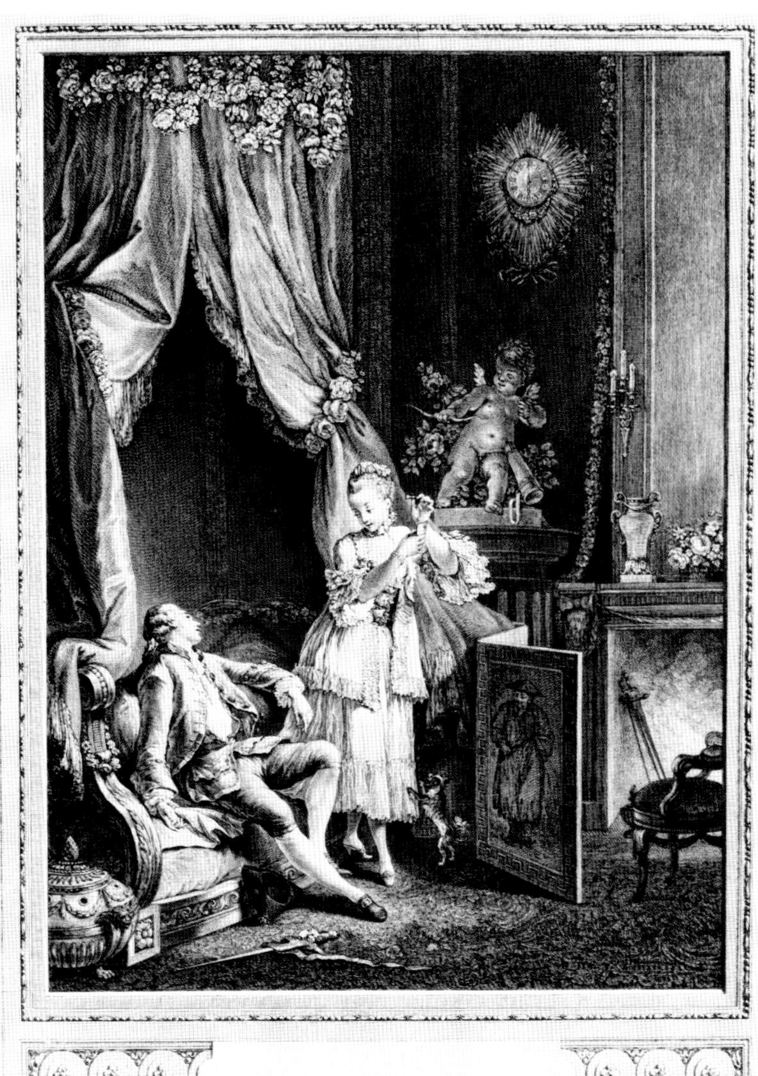
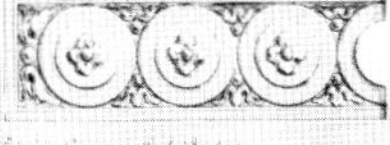
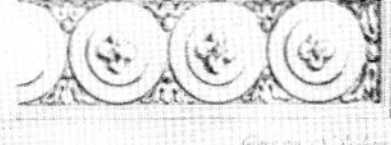

CLARE LEIGHTON
American, b. England, 1901
The Tranter's Party, 1937–40, from Thomas Hardy, *Under the Greenwood Tree, or the Mellstock Quire* (New York, 1940)
Wood engraving, proof
Gift of the Still Water Foundation, 1987

CLARE LEIGHTON
American, b. England, 1901
Lobstering, 1940–50, from twelve designs of New England industries for Wedgewood Plates
Wood engraving, 42/50
Gift of the Still Water Foundation, 1987

ALEXANDRE-LOUIS LELOIR
French, 1843–1884
Moroccan Girl Playing Stringed Instrument, 1875
Watercolor
Gift of the Wunsch Foundation, Inc., 1983.133

FRANÇOIS LEMOINE
French, 1688–1737
Dido and Aeneas, n.d.
Black pencil and black chalk heightened with white on blue paper
Archer M. Huntington Museum Fund, 1984.77

LANCE LETSCHER
American, 1962–
Large Crown of Thorns, 1987
Drypoint and photo-lithograph on chine collé over organic material
Archer M. Huntington Museum Fund, 1987.40

DAVID LUCAS
English, 1802–1881
A Lock on the Stour,
after John Constable, 1831
Mezzotint
Archer M. Huntington Museum
Fund, 1985.4

ARMANDO MORALES
Nicaraguan, 1927–
Desundo en frente de espejo concavo
(Nude in Front of Concave Mirror),
1980
Eight-color lithograph, proof, IX/
XV
Gift of Gene and Dana Ravel,
1987.8

ELIZABETH MURRAY
American, 1940–
Untitled, 1982
Fifteen-color screenprint
in three parts, 15/50
Archer M. Huntington Museum
Fund, 1986.162

JOSÉ CLEMENTE OROZCO
Mexican, 1883–1949
Teatro de variedades en Harlem
(Vaudeville in Harlem), 1928
Lithograph, edition unknown
Archer M. Huntington Museum
Fund, 1986.89

JOSÉ CLEMENTE OROZCO
Mexican, 1883–1949
El fraile y el indio
(The Franciscan and the Indian),
1930
Lithograph, unnumbered/100
Archer M. Huntington Museum
Fund, 1986.87

ROBERT RAUSCHENBERG
American, 1925–
Treaty, 1974
Color lithograph on two sheets,
12/31
Archer M. Huntington Museum
Fund, 1987.85

REMBRANDT VAN RIJN
Dutch, 1606–1669
Clement De Jonghe,
Printseller, 1651
Etching, drypoint and burin, v/vi
Archer M. Huntington Museum
Fund, 1987.87

DIEGO RIVERA
Mexican, 1886–1957
Still Life, 1918
Pencil
Archer M. Huntington Museum
Fund, 1986.76

DIEGO RIVERA
Mexican, 1886–1957
Russian Dock Worker, 1928
Watercolor and pencil
on graph paper
Archer M. Huntington Museum
Fund, 1986.74

DIEGO RIVERA
Mexican, 1886–1957
Seated Nude, 1929
Charcoal
Archer M. Huntington Museum
Fund, 1986.75

DIEGO RIVERA
Mexican, 1886–1957
Nude, Frida Kahlo, 1930
Lithograph, 93/100
Archer M. Huntington Museum
Fund, 1986.73

DIEGO RIVERA
Mexican, 1886–1957
Nude, Frida Kahlo, 1930
Lithograph, unnumbered proof
Archer M. Huntington Museum
Fund, 1986.103

DIEGO RIVERA
Mexican, 1886–1957
La maestra rural
(The Rural School Teacher), 1932
Lithograph, 96/100
Archer M. Huntington Museum
Fund, 1986.100

AUGUSTIN DE SAINT-
AUBIN
French, 1736–1807
A Reception at the Hôtel de Ville,
Paris, ca. 1775–85
Grey wash over black chalk with
touches of pen and ink
Archer M. Huntington Museum
Fund, 1987.14

DAVID ÁLFARO SIQUERIOS
Mexican, 1896–1974
Zapata, 1930
Lithograph, edition unknown
Archer M. Huntington Museum
Fund, 1986.77

DAVID ÁLFARO SIQUERIOS
Mexican, 1896–1974
Portrait of Moises Saenz, 1931
Lithograph, edition unknown
Archer M. Huntington Museum
Fund, 1986.55

STEVEN SORMAN
American, 1948–
West Union/Sabbathday Lake, 1982
Two-color lithograph, 8/41
Archer M. Huntington Museum
Fund, 1987.58

RAPHAEL SOYER
American, 1899–1987
Study of a Female Nude, n.d.
Watercolor over pencil
Gift of Latane Temple,
1985.121

12. GIOVANNI BATTISTA GAULLI, called Baciccio, Italian, 1639–1709, *Study of a Woman's Head and Hands*, ca. 1675–80, red chalk on beige paper, Friends of the Archer M. Huntington Art Gallery Purchase, 1987.16.

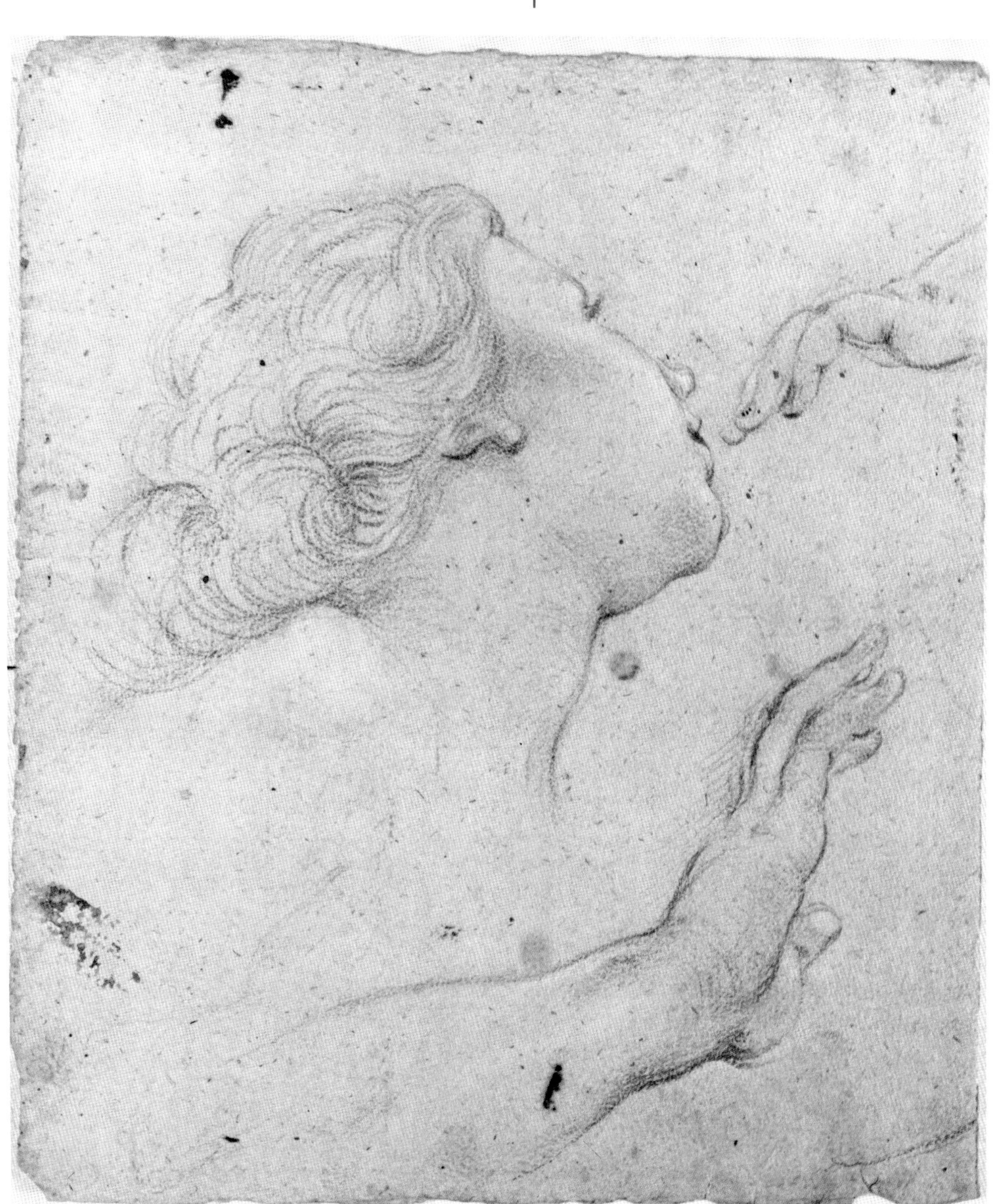

13. FRANÇOIS-MARIUS GRANET, French, 1775–1849, *Monks Entering a Cloister*, ca. 1802–19, pen and brown ink with brown and grey washes on off-white paper, Archer M. Huntington Museum Fund, 1987.18.

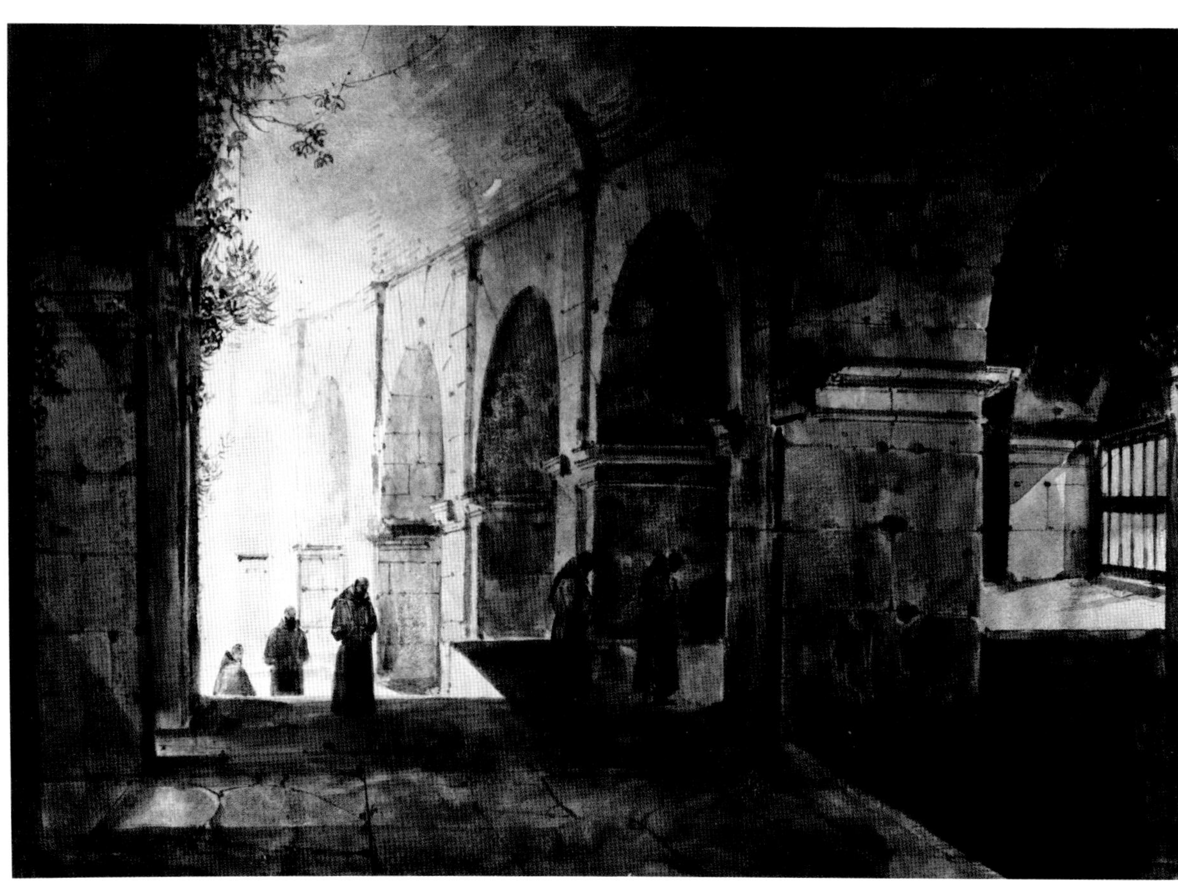

DONALD SULTAN
American, 1951–
Black Lemons (three lemons), 1987
Aquatint, 5/14
Archer M. Huntington Museum Fund, 1987.44

JAMES SURLS
American, 1943–
See across the See, 1986
Lithograph, U.T. edition, V/V
Transfer from the Guest Artists in Printmaking Program, Art Department,
The University of Texas at Austin, 1986.154

JAMES JACQUES TISSOT
French, 1836–1902
Le banc de jardin
(*The Garden Bench*), 1883
Mezzotint, i/iii
Archer M. Huntington Museum Fund, 1986.6

PATRICIA VARGAS
Chilean, 20th C.
Untitled, 1981
Mixed media
Archer M. Huntington Museum Fund, 1983.113

AGOSTINO DEI MUSI, called AGOSTINO VENEZIANO
Italian, act. 1514–36
The Israelites Gathering Mannah from Heaven, after Raphael, ca. 1520–25
Engraving, only state
Archer M. Huntington Museum Fund, 1987.46

ROBERT WILSON
American, 1941–
"Alceste", Act II SC.1, 1986
Lithograph, 20/20
Transfer from the Guest Artists in Printmaking Program, Art Department,
The University of Texas at Austin, 1986.145

ROBERT WILSON
American, 1941–
Einstein Chair, 1977
Etching, 15/15
Archer M. Huntington Museum Fund, 1987.83

1. ANONYMOUS (Circle of the Taranto Painter), Greek, *Corinthian Stemless Cup (Kylix)*, 590–580 B.C., clay, The Lillian and C.W. Duncan Foundation, Dr. & Mrs. George Kozmetsky, Archer M. Huntington Museum Fund, 1984.39.

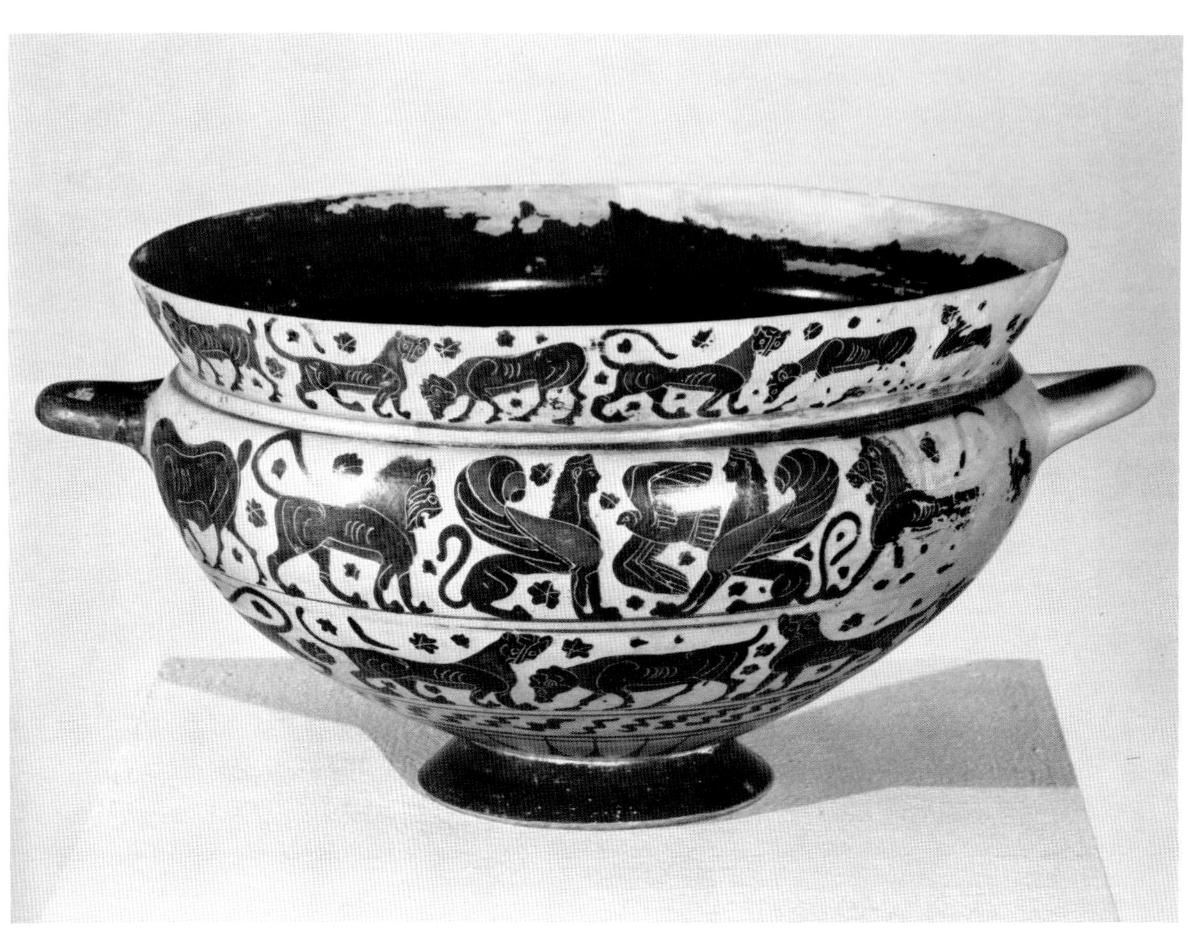

ANCIENT AND EUROPEAN ART

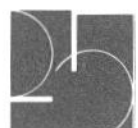

"The time has passed when a major collection of European art can be formed; there are no more fine paintings available except at impossible prices." This statement represents a widely held belief among collectors, curators, and museum directors in the United States today. A major collector of Old Master drawings told me a few years years ago that it was pointless to imagine that a museum could form an Old Master collection in this age, since all the major works were either already in public collections or prohibitively expensive. Everywhere one hears that the age of museum collecting of historical Western art is rapidly drawing to a close, since most of the works are already in public hands, too expensive for any but the most stupendous budgets, or unexportable. Surprisingly, the idea is not a new one. In 1908, the head of the Minneapolis School of Art told the board of trustees of the newly formed Minneapolis Institute of Arts that it was too late to begin a collection of European art and that the new museum should instead devote itself to early and modern American art. Even in 1815 a French art critic felt it necessary to argue against the common belief that there were no longer any older masterpieces to be found on the market.[1]

With the mandate of a distinguished panel of museum directors, the administration of the Huntington Art Gallery decided to challenge this proposition and begin to expand the collections at The University of Texas to represent the full range of world art. A propitious occasion for this project was the sale in the summer of 1980 at Christie's in London of the Castle Ashby collection of ancient vases. The Huntington purchased 13 vases, creating in one move both a collection where none had been before and a gap to fill, since there was nothing on permanent display between the end of antiquity and the mid-nineteenth century.

A collection of ancient art was a high priority for the museum. First, ancient art has a large constituency on campus. Two professors teach ancient art history, and the classics department is an important one in Texas, with many professors who use original artifacts in their courses. Second, the prices of fine antiquities were still fairly reasonable, so that the purchase of one would not exhaust the entire fund for a year. The initial purchase of vases was supported by several acquisitions each year, of vases or marble, bronze, and terracotta sculpture. Now that a collection has been established, the goal is to purchase approximately one work a year.

The breadth of the collection, which consisted initially of Athenian and South Italian vases and a few marble sculptures, has increased in recent years through the addition of several works in bronze and terracottta, and a large vase from Corinth. In 1983 the museum purchased a bronze belt from Urartu, an area between the Caspian and Black Seas, where Mount Ararat is located. The belt was made during the seventh century before Christ, after Urartu had been conquered by the neighboring Assyrians. Urartians are noted for their bronzes, like this one, in which the Assyrian animal designs are handled with particular fluency and skill. The Huntington belt, with its subtle handling of animal forms and fluid modelling, is perhaps the finest quality Urartian belt known. These animal patterns are characteristic of the "orientalizing" style of the art of Greece and Italy during the eighth and seventh centuries B.C.

Shortly after the acquisition of the belt, the Huntington acquired a Corinthian cup (fig. 1), where something of the influence of Urartu can be seen in the animals which

2. ANONYMOUS, Greek (Hellenistic), *Dancing Figure*, 2nd-1st C., B.C., bronze, Frost Bros. Benefit and Archer M. Huntington Museum Fund, 1986.46.

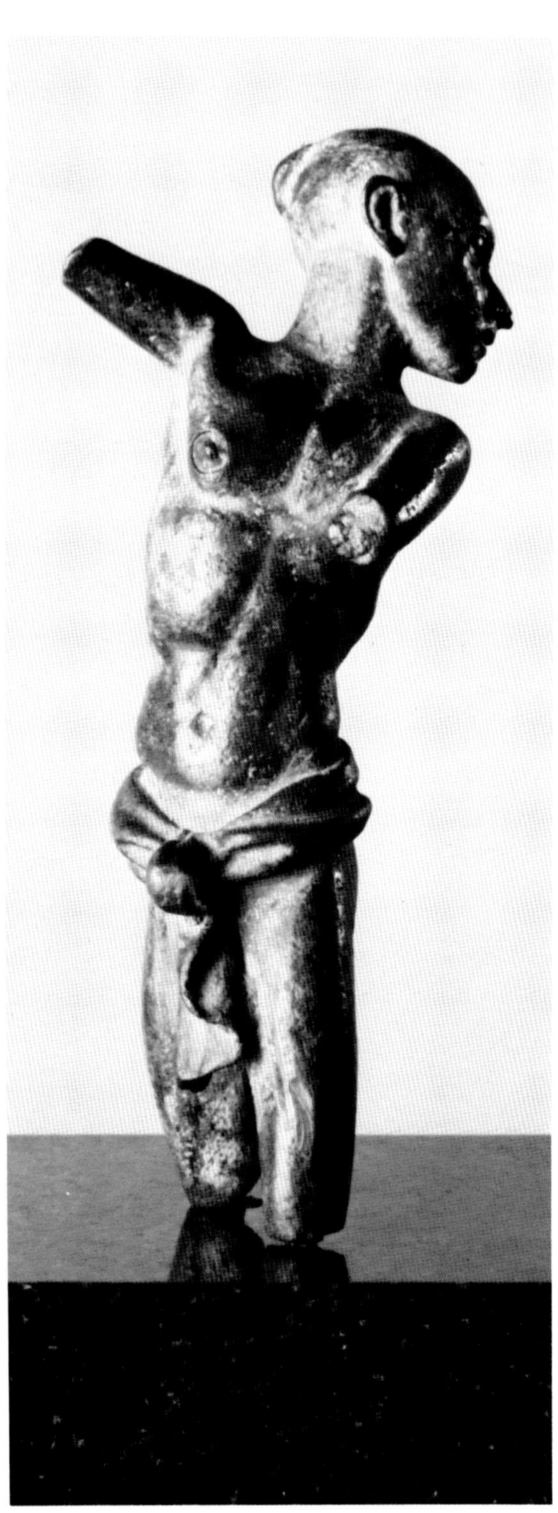

circle it in rings. The cup's stemless, deep-bowled shape and the black-figure animals arranged in rows on a buff background date it to the Middle Corinthian period (600–575 B.C.). The irregularly incised rosettes and spirited yet detailed handling of the animals have been associated with the style of an artist known as the Taranto Painter.[2] The frieze of animals on the rim of the Huntington cup is unique; all other cups of this type have plain rims. With a small Corinthian aryballos already in the collection, this cup represents an important style of ancient ceramic work. The Corinthian cup was purchased with the help of the Lillian and C.W. Duncan Foundation and Dr. and Mrs. George Kozmetsky.

The first ancient bronze to enter the collection was purchased in 1984. It is a personification of Autumn as a small boy (putto), holding a cornucopia of grapes. As is common with ancient bronzes, he once had silver eyes. In 1986 the opportunity arose to complement this bronze with a striking and important Hellenistic *Dancing Figure* (fig. 2), which may well be the best object in the ancient collection. This figure, identified as a Nubian slave, not only displays a remarkably twisting body, encouraging the viewer to walk around him in order to see him completely, but also has a facial expression of striking pathos. The small form encapsulates all the emotionalism, exoticism, and complex movement of Hellenistic art.

The collection contains a number of South Italian vases, including two from Canosa and Centuripe which incorporate female figures on their handles or spouts. In 1984 we were able to acquire, with funds from Dennis R. and Elmer Kapp, five independent female terracotta figurines, examples of the figurines that could be found in ancient temples, households, and tombs. Their buff coarse-

3. GIOVANNI FRANCESCO BARBIERI, called Il Guercino, Italian, 1591–1666, *Astrology*, ca. 1650's, oil on canvas, Archer M. Huntington Museum Fund, 1984.57.

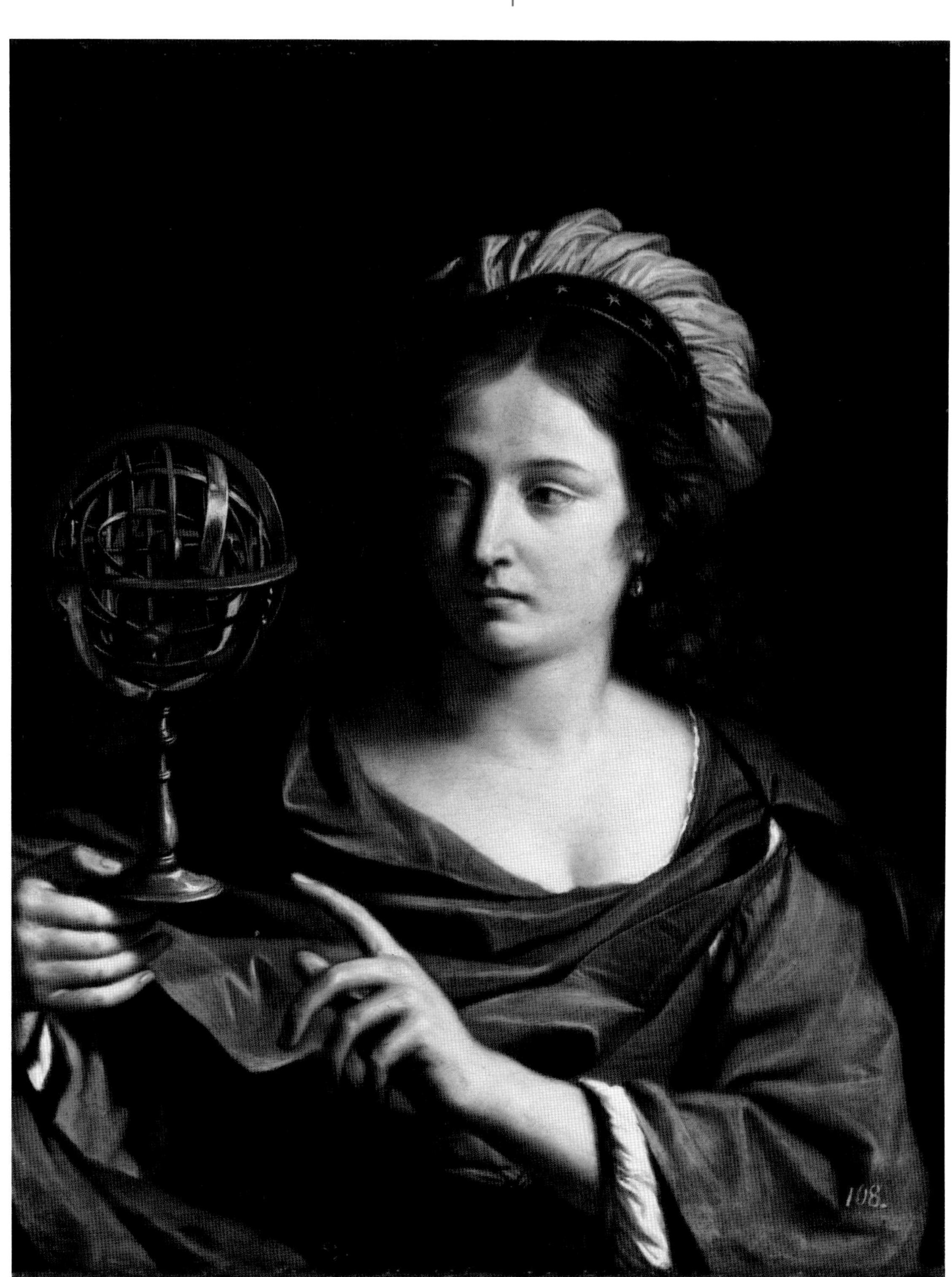

4. FRANCESCO SALVATOR FONTEBASSO, Italian, 1709–1769, *Adoration of the Magi*, 18th C., oil on canvas, Frost Bros. Benefit and Archer M. Huntington Museum Fund, 1985.18.

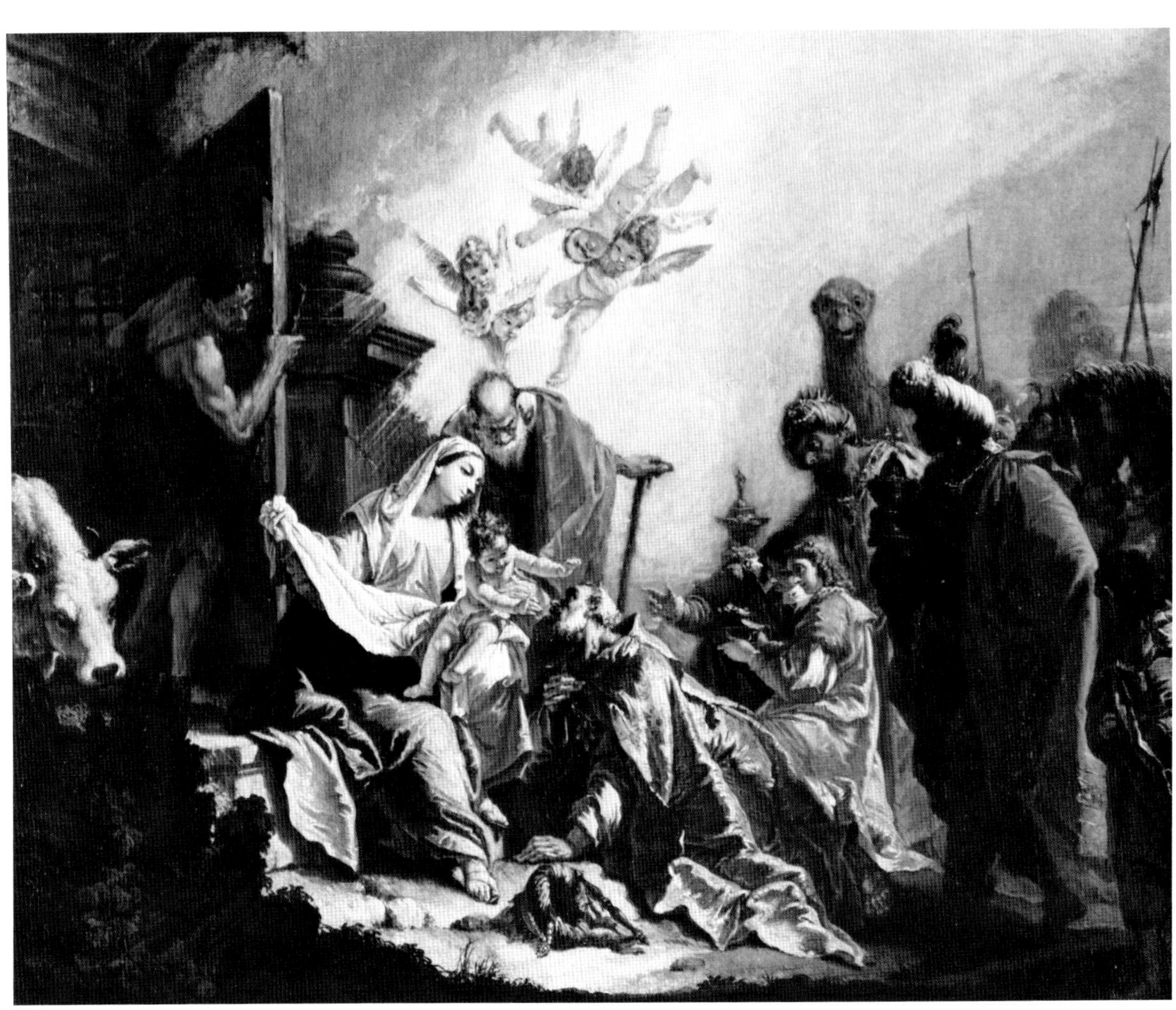

5. ALEXANDER ARCHIPENKO, Russian, 1887–1964, *Egyptian Motif*, 1917, bronze, Friends of the Archer M. Huntington Art Gallery Purchase, 1983.64.

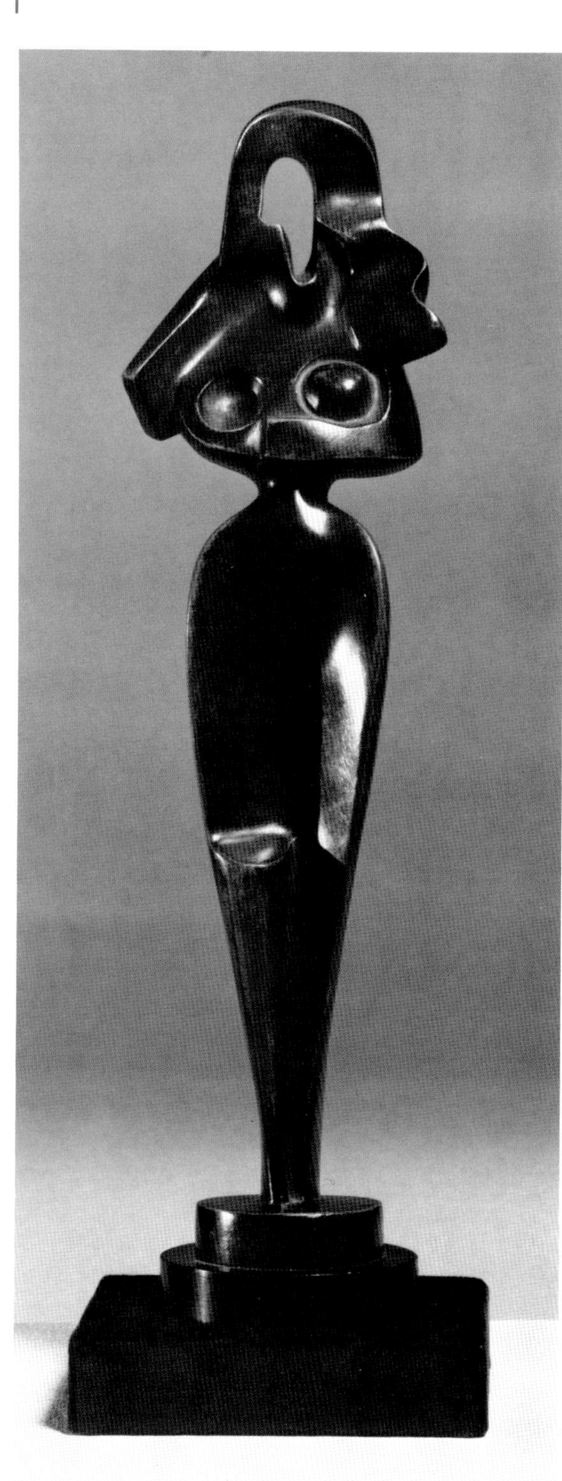

grained clay is typical of Apulian terracottas. Like one of our vases, these are probably from Canosa, and may well have been recovered from one of the large underground tombs excavated there.[3] The figures were cast from molds; in fact, the three larger figures were probably cast from the same mold.

Another priority for collecting was European art, and in 1984 the university administration approved the acquisition of six European paintings of the sixteenth and seventeenth centuries. One of these, *Astrology* (fig. 3) by Giovanni Francesco Barbieri, called Il Guercino, is exhibited here. *Astrology* wears a headdress encircled with stars and holds an armillary sphere. With its strong contrasts between light and shade, its simple composition and classicizing female figure, the painting represents the baroque classicism of Guercino's later style.

Shortly after the arrival of these first six European paintings, the gallery received a remarkable gift, a French panel painting depicting St. Bernard of Clairvaux, the founder of the Cistercian monastic order. The artist is unknown, but the work probably dates from the late fifteenth century. It is probably the right panel of a diptych; the Madonna would have been depicted on the left panel. The detailed articulation of the saint's face makes this an excellent example of Northern European painting of the early Renaissance.

The first Frost Bros. benefit supported the acquisition of the Huntington's first eighteenth-century Italian painting. Francesco Fontebasso's *Adoration of the Magi* (fig. 4) is one of the artist's masterpieces, and an excellent example of the vivacity of Venetian painting under the influence of Tiepolo. Also purchased in 1985 was Hans Rottenhammer's *Adoration of the Shepherds*, one of two paintings on copper in the collection, and an example of work by a Northern European artist who spent a considerable amount of time in Italy. Rottenhammer's figures and composition show the strong influence of Italian painting on his work.

The Huntington Art Gallery owns very little twentieth-century European painting and sculpture, but a few works have been acquired in recent years. The Friends of the Huntington voted in 1983 to acquire a bronze sculpture by Alexander Archipenko, cast after a model he made in Paris in 1917. The bronze, *Egyptian Motif* (fig. 5), manifests the influence of cubism on sculpture. In 1986 the daughter of Tamara DeLempicka generously donated four paintings by her mother, representing the full span of the career of this fascinating European artist, who lived much of her later life in the United States and Mexico. *Le Modele*, a reworking of a painting of 1925, also reflects the influence of cubism on early twentieth century art.

Despite auspicious beginnings, the Huntington collections continue to have major gaps. We own no medieval art, for example. Our ancient collection is in need of major works of sculpture (more portraits, a major relief, a full-sized figure or torso), of a vase by a name painter, and of a geometric vase. In Old Master painting we lack French painting after 1500, Italian Renaissance art, and representation of most of the later Italian schools. We own virtually no Spanish or English painting, and no European sculpture besides the Archipenko and our Rodin. We need representation of virtually every aspect of European modern and contemporary art. Most of these works are still available on the art market today. With concerted effort, the gaps can be substantially narrowed, to continue to make the collection function successfully for the teaching of art and the edification of visitors to the museum.

Andrea S. Norris
Chief Curator

[1]Michael Conforti, "Introduction," *The Art of Collecting: Acquisitions at the Minneapolis Institute of Arts 1980–1985* (Minneapolis, 1986), 10.

[2]Debra Schafter, art history paper, Fall, 1987.
I am grateful to Kendall Curlee for sharing this and the following source with me.

[3]Anne Johns, graduate art history paper, Fall, 1987.

ANCIENT AND EUROPEAN ART

ANONYMOUS
Greek (Hellenistic)
Dancing Figure, 2nd-1st C., B.C.
Bronze
Frost Bros. Benefit and
Archer M. Huntington Museum
Fund, 1986.46

ANONYMOUS
Roman
Figure of Autumn, 1st C., B.C.–
1st C., A.D.
Bronze
Archer M. Huntington Museum
Fund, 1984.79

ANONYMOUS
French
Portrait of St. Bernard, 15th C.
Oil on board
Gift of Charles and Loretta
Marsh, 1984.105

ANONYMOUS (CIRCLE OF
THE TARANTO PAINTER)
Greek
Corinthian Stemless Cup (Kylix),
590–580 B.C.
Clay
The Lillian and C. W. Duncan
Foundation,
Dr. & Mrs. George Kozmetsky,
Archer M. Huntington Museum
Fund, 1984.39

ANONYMOUS
South Italian
*Standing Female Figure, Perhaps
Venus*,
3rd C., B.C.
Terracotta
Purchased as a gift of Dennis R.
and Elmer Kapp, 1984.103

ANONYMOUS
South Italian
*Seated Winged Figure, Perhaps
a Nike*, 3rd C., B.C.
Terracotta
Purchased as a gift of Dennis R.
and Elmer Kapp, 1984.104

ANONYMOUS
Urartian
Belt, 650–600 C., B.C.
Bronze
Archer M. Huntington Museum
Fund, 1983.124

ALEXANDER ARCHIPENKO
Russian, 1887–1964
Egyptain Motif, 1917
Bronze
Friends of the Archer M.
Huntington Art Gallery
Purchase,
1983.64

TAMARA DE LEMPICKA
Polish, 1898–1980
Le Modèle
Oil on canvas
Gift of Kizette de Lempicka
Foxhall, 1986.175

FRANCESCO SALVATOR
FONTEBASSO
Italian, 1709–1769
Adoration of the Magi, 18th C.
Oil on canvas
Frost Bros. Benefit and
Archer M. Huntington Museum
Fund, 1985.18

GIOVANNI FRANCESCO
BARBIERI,
called Il Guercino
Italian, 1591–1666
Astrology, ca. 1650's
Oil on canvas
Archer M. Huntington Museum
Fund, 1984.57

HANS ROTTENHAMMER
German, 1564–1625
The Adoration of the Shepherds,
ca. 1600
Oil on copper
Archer M. Huntington Museum
Fund, 1985.69

DECORATIVE ARTS

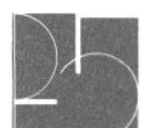

In the United States, art museums have collected decorative arts primarily since the latter half of the nineteenth century. As this movement grew and museums in the early twentieth century began to expand their collections, a variety of media and periods were included: ancient, medieval and ethnographic arts, western sculpture and textiles, and the traditional decorative arts of furniture, ceramics, silver and glass. As the Metropolitan, Philadelphia, and Cleveland Museums of Art, and the Minneapolis and Detroit Institutes of Art, among others, began to focus on the decorative arts, entire rooms with wall paneling, floors, ceilings and all the accompanying accoutrements created what are now called Period Rooms.

At the Huntington, since the history of collecting is so new and various divisions are just now emerging in the museum's long-term mission, the collecting of decorative arts until the last eight years had been, for the most part, nonexistent. Since 1980, however, textiles, sculpture, ancient and medieval arts, along with painting, have been combined into the general category called European art, and only now are certain strengths emerging in the more traditional forms of painting and sculpture themselves.

Because the Huntington's mission specifies that the museum will work with all academic departments at The University of Texas at Austin, and since one of its most active users has been the School of Architecture with its various related departments, several years ago it was decided to collect a type of furniture which would best serve not only their teaching needs, but provide scholarly research potential for other academic departments as well. After long deliberation, the chair was selected as the most useful, least sizeable, and most consistent form with which to show the evolution of stylistic change and period, and one which would mirror the development of architecture from the beginning of the New World. Since style, history, and interior architecture are all related to each other in the study of decorative arts, the chair itself has become a superb first object with which to teach these many diverse, but interrelated, concepts. By beginning with Flemish and English antecedents, the collection of chairs, both American and European, with their corresponding stylistic developments, now enables faculty in architecture, interior architecture, home economics, history and art history to teach a variety of related pursuits.

In developing this collection, one which is on-going and is very much incomplete, it is the museum's intention to acquire chairs which show stylistic regional differences, as evidenced in major cultural cities beginning with the early eighteenth century. Charleston, Philadelphia, Baltimore, New York, Boston and Rhode Island were centers each with their own styles. As American architecture evolved and all of the revivals became dominant in the nineteenth century, artistic design and workmanship moved from the hand-made to the mass produced. This, too, is reflected in the collection with chairs by Gustav Stickley and Frank Lloyd Wright in the early twentieth century, and continues to this day with mass-produced chairs from the fifties to the present. Many of the most recent acquisitions show influences from earlier periods, not only American but also European.

With 31 chairs now in the collection, the long-term acquisition plan established by the Director in conjunction with various academic units now has a teaching nucleus and the support of several decorative arts advo-

ANONYMOUS, American, 18th C., *William and Mary Bannister Back Side Chair*, ca. 1720, wood and rush, gift of the Wunsch Americana Foundation, 1986.45.

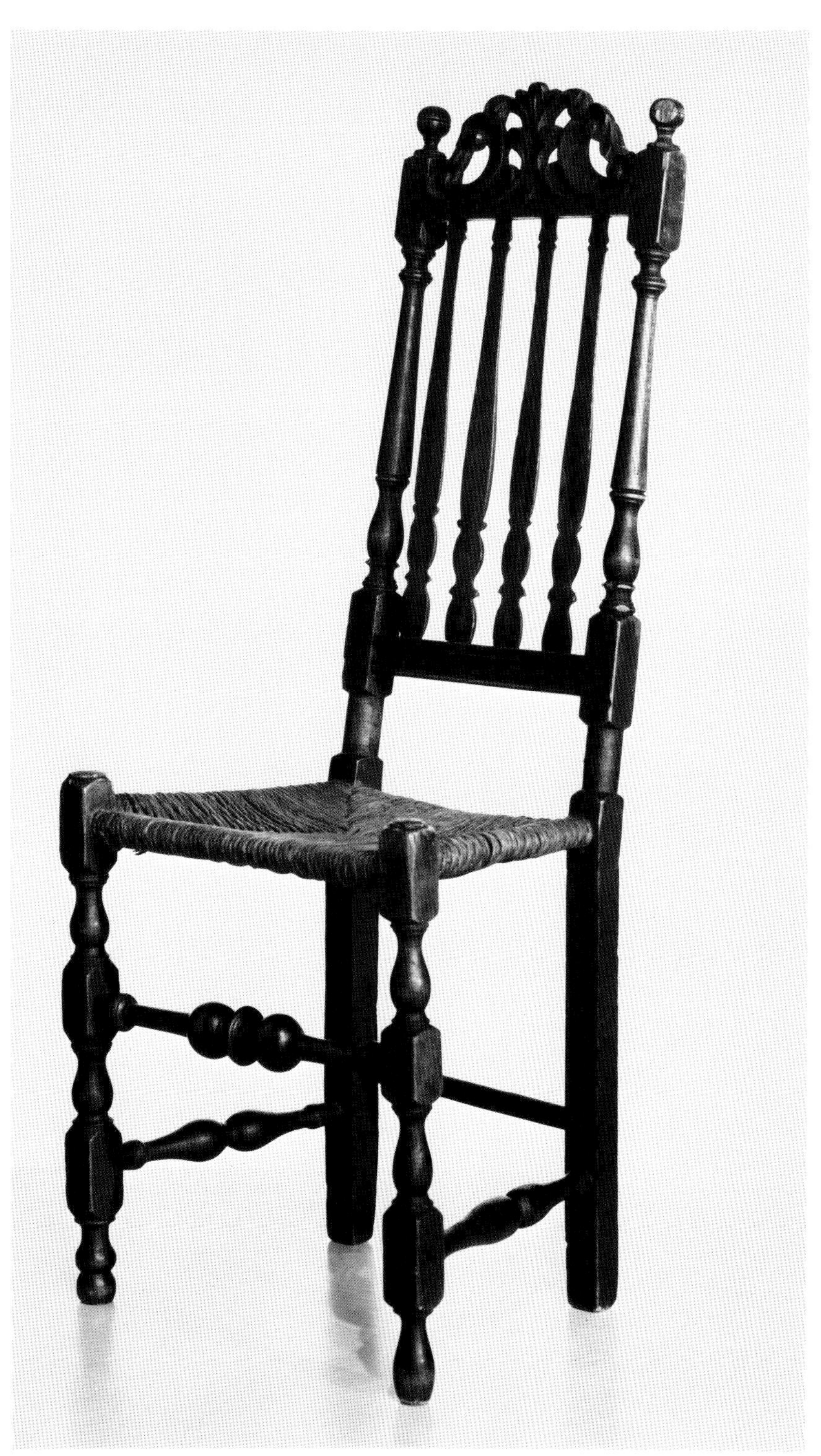

FRANK LLOYD WRIGHT
American, 1867–1959, *Side Chair*, ca. 1908, Oak with upholstered seat, Archer M. Huntington Museum Fund, 1983.47

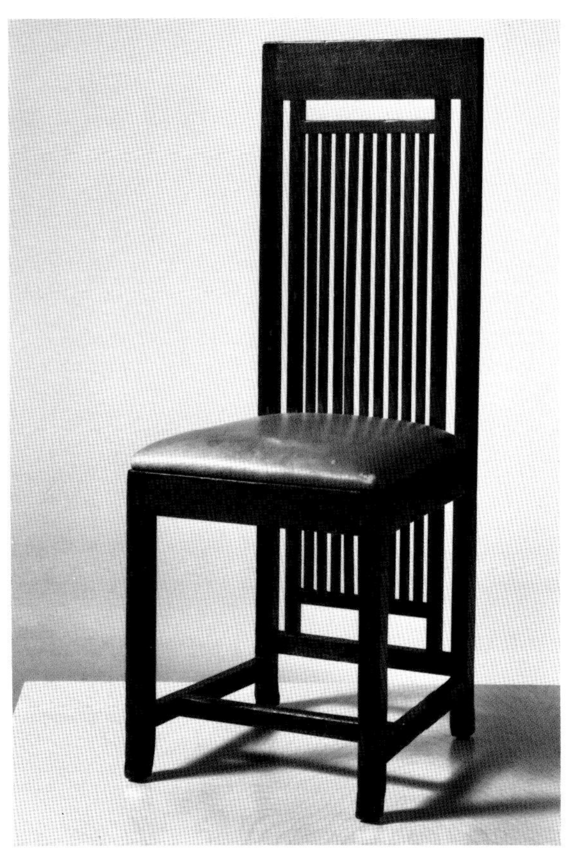

cates. Specifically, the seventeenth through early nineteenth century have grown through the generosity of Mr. Eric Martin Wunsch, New York City and twentieth century additions have come primarily from Mr. & Mrs. Meredith Long, Houston. Their interest in the understanding of the importance of the decorative arts in the teaching of American art history has been crucial and the Huntington's collection, for the most part, exists because of their collective vision.

Although the majority of the decorative arts collection focuses on the chair, other related objects have come to the Museum in this field, including textiles, ceramics, and glass. These are extremely limited, and do not enable any kind of comprehensive teaching to be done at this time. Furthermore, silver, which also reflects much stylistic change throughout history specifically in Europe and America, is not at all represented. Hopefully, future donors will make possible the expansion of the decorative arts collection in these media in addition to helping expand the chair collection itself.

Because of space limitations, the collection has focused primarily on the decorative arts in North America. Eventually this must be expanded to include European antecedents so that a full, broad, comprehensive explanation of the evolution of these forms can be taught. Sculpture and textiles are almost non-existent in the permanent collection, and these omissions also must be addressed in the future.

Museum professionals and museumgoers are often surprised and enriched when far-sighted individuals collect broadly in unfashionable areas. To acquire unpopular work at a time when the market is low means that truly wonderful collections can be developed and in place when popular fashion and trends catch up. Since the Huntington is a comprehensive art museum, the only one of its type in Central Texas, greatly expanded collections are important for the education of all people in the region. If we neglect entire periods, countries, and style, future generations in Central Texas will suffer for the lack of it. Although opportunities in the marketplace are usually financially limiting, focused attention by interested people always can make things possible.

Eric S. McCready
Director

CHARLES EAMES (American, 1907–1978) and Ray Eames (American, 20th C.), *LCW Chair*, 1946, molded and bent birch, gift of Meredith and Cornelia Long, 1983.127.

ANONYMOUS
American
New York Klismos Chair,
ca. 1815–1825
Mahogany and upholstery
Archer M. Huntington Museum
Fund, 1986.49

ANONYMOUS
American, 18th C.
William and Mary Bannister Back Side Chair, ca. 1720
Wood and rush
Gift of the Wunsch Americana
Foundation, 1986.45

CHARLES EAMES
(1907–1978)
RAY EAMES (20th C.)
American
LCW Chair, designed 1946
Molded and bent birch
Gift of Meredith and Cornelia
Long, 1983.127

SOTTSASS ASSOCIATI
Italian, founded 1980
Lodge Armchair, 1981
Steel, chrome and wood
upholstery
Archer M. Huntington Museum
Fund, 1987

FRANK LLOYD WRIGHT
American, 1867–1959
Side Chair, ca. 1908
Oak with upholstered seat
Archer M. Huntington Museum
Fund, 1983.47

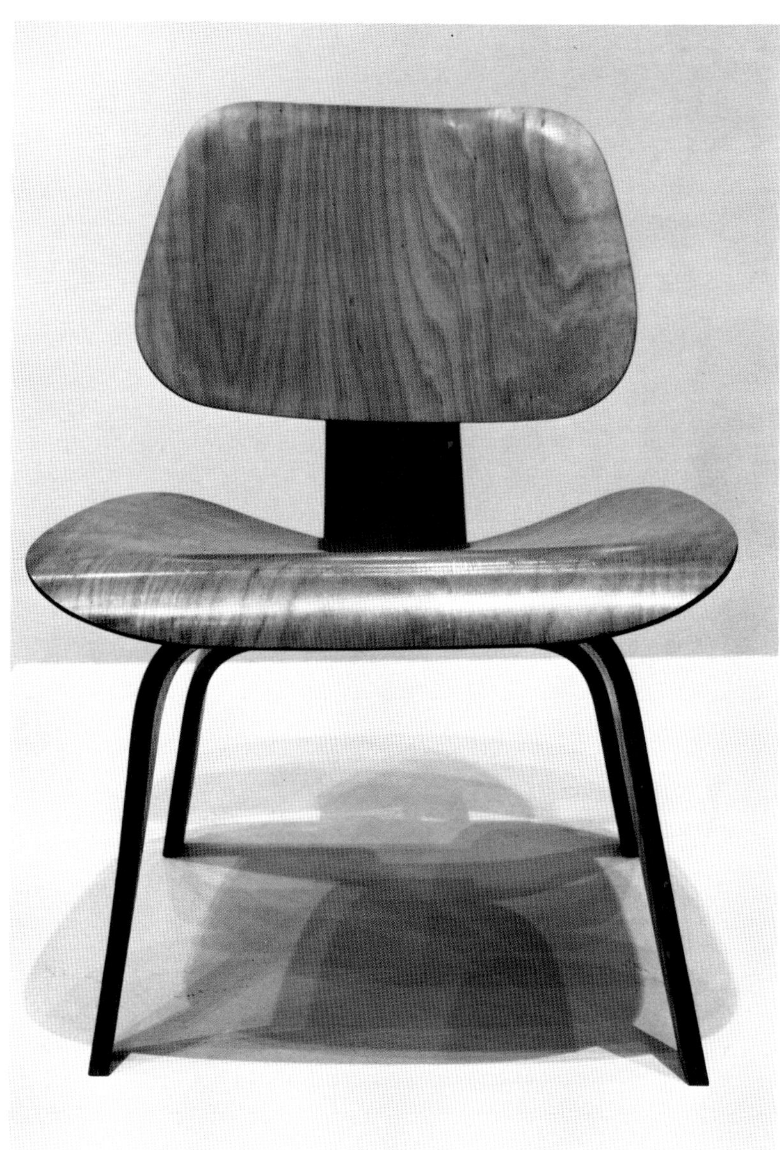

ARCHER M. HUNTINGTON ART GALLERY STAFF

Eric S. McCready	Director
Lynne Adele	Administrative Assistant
Pony Allen	Technical Staff Assistant
Eric Anderson	Technical Staff Assistant
Jonathan Bober	Curator of Prints and Drawings
Cecilia Carter	Senior Office Assistant
Ellie Francis	Administrative Assistant
JoAnn Goodman	Administrative Assistant
Patricia Hendricks	Associate Curator
Jessie Otto Hite	Assistant Director of Public Affairs
Clyde Holleman	Carpenter
George Holmes	Photographer
Sue Ellen Jeffers	Registrar
Robert Jones	Technical Staff Supervisor
Susan Mayer	Education Coordinator
Andrea Norris	Chief Curator
Fran Prudhomme	Art Enrichment Coordinator
Becky Duval Reese	Assistant Director for Public Programs
Tim Reilly	Technical Staff Assistant
Jill Robertson	Assistant Registrar
John Sager	Technical Staff Assistant
Jane Scroggs	Friends Coordinator
Susan Sternberg	Tour Coordinator/Program Specialist
Donna Vliet	Art Teacher, Art Enrichment Program
Tanya Walker	Administrative Associate
David Willard	Manager of Publicity, Promotions, and Public Relations

George Holmes	Photography
Barbara Jezek	Design
G&S Typesetters Inc.	Typography
Whitley Co.	Printing